A History of Roads

A HISTORY OF ROADS

Geoffrey Hindley

THE CITADEL PRESS
SECAUCUS, NEW JERSEY

First American edition, 1972
Copyright © 1971 by Geoffrey Hindley
All rights reserved
Published by Citadel Press, Inc.
A subsidiary of Lyle Stuart, Inc.
120 Enterprise Ave., Secaucus, N.J. 07094
Manufactured in the United States of America
Library of Congress catalog card number: 12-85520
ISBN 0-8065-0290-8

Contents

Illustrations

(Between pages 54 and 55)

Plate

1   An ancient Roman road

2   One of the tombs lining the Via Appia

3   A Royal Mail coach

4   James Whitney, highwayman

5   A British wagon, 1808

6   A pavier at work

7   The old toll-gate at Notting Hill

8   Celebrating the abolition of turnpike gates at Devizes, 1868

9   Italian highwaymen in action

10   The approach to the Mont Cenis pass

11   The St Gotthard mail coach

12   A natural bridge on one of the ancient Navajo trails

13   An American wagon train

14   The turnpike at Harrodsburg, Kentucky, 1885

15   Conditions on the road between Cleveland and Warrenville, Ohio, 1891

(Between pages 102 and 103)

16   A German autobahn of the 1930s

17   A 1934 advertisement on the autostrada to Pompeii

18   Building one of the autobahns in Germany in the 1930s

19   The Glossglocknerstrasse under construction in 1963

Maps

Author's Note

The history of roads is also the history of the traffic that has travelled over them and the communities by which they were built. In this book I have aimed to indicate the general lines of development in the history of the world's overland transport and to link this with the nature of the societies that constructed and used the roads. It is not a technical book; the reader will find in the book list some pointers to the large literature on road-building, the problems of road administration and finance, and the whole field of civil engineering as related to overland transport. However, I hope that the expert in these fields will find this a useful general survey to supplement his specialist studies and that the layman will enjoy it as an introduction to an interesting and important subject.

I should like to thank the following for kind permission to reproduce the illustrations: The Mansell Collection (Plates 1-18); Keystone Press Agency Ltd (Plates 19-22, 27, 29); Japan Information Centre, London (Plates 23, 24); Thomson Newspapers Ltd (Plates 25, 26, 28).

I owe a debt also to Miss Diane Dancklefsen who kindly prepared the maps.

G. H.

Introduction

M AN HAS ALWAYS been a traveller. In the centuries before the revolutionary discovery and perfection of agricultural techniques the nomadic hunting tribes of early man followed familiar and well-trodden routes from one camping ground to another and from the summer to the winter territory. In some cases they followed the migratory routes of animals, but always they were in search of the easiest route—following a direct line across plain open country, the contours of the land in hilly country and the course of a river or a cleared path in wooded country. In many areas of the world roads remained little more than beaten tracks right up to the eighteenth century of the Christian era, and indeed they often covered prehistoric routes.

The first 'roads' traced the wanderings of early tribes, but in this survey, which spans some five thousand years from the neolithic ways of ancient Europe to the multi-lane expressways of modern America, a road is considered to be a route of overland communication between established communities. The tracks followed by the walk-abouts of the Aborigines of Australia are not to our purpose, nor is the short but important trackway used by the massive vehicle which takes the Saturn rocket to the launching pad. Both serve essentially one-way journeys, neither carries the two-way traffic implied in the word 'communication'. A road, then, is not to be defined by the nature of its surface—most of the trade and postal service of the ancient world travelled over unmade tracks—but rather by its function and the nature of the traffic that travels over it. In fact, throughout history the road and its traffic have been but two faces of the same coin, the one affecting the design of the other in the most direct way.

In planning the road of the motor age the engineer and surveyor increasingly find themselves faced with wide-ranging problems of environmental planning; the extent to which they and the planners recognise the close links between the roads and the community they serve has implications far beyond the ease of movement of the road-user. In our own generation the expansion of all methods of communications, the pressure of population increases, and the generally rising standard of individual wealth are producing a degree of urban sprawl in the more advanced countries of the world that threatens to eliminate altogether the age-old concept of a community as a distinct entity. In this radical change of attitudes the motor-car and the roads that serve it are of central import-ance. From being service links between communities roads are, in our own day, threatening to destroy them both literally and figuratively.

The modern motorway is an extreme example of the road being adapted to the requirements of the traffic it is to carry. Although the principle is not of course new, it was only comparatively recently that it was adapted as axiomatic by European road-planners. For a long time effort was devoted to designing vehicles adapted to the road conditions and, in the absence of any serious public investment in road-building, such an attitude was understandable. As late as the 1960s a French company produced a car fitted with an hydraulic mechanism that allowed the driver to alter the height of the car above the road, depending on the quality of the surface.

The earliest routes to be dealt with in this book were for pedestrian traffic. In consequence we shall see that many of the neolithic routes of ancient Europe followed the high contours of chalk or other well-drained uplands, even though the settlements which they linked might lie in valleys. The steep ascent to the uplands, although perhaps tiring to a walking man, was perfectly feasible and the advantages of dry ground under foot for the greater part of the journey far outweighed the rigours of the climb. With the coming of the use of draught animals such as the ox and the horse, another of the fruits of the neolithic revolution, the matter of gradient became somewhat more important, as did that of the surfacing of the road. At a surprisingly early date we find traces of arti-ficial road surfaces, which suggests that as soon as Man had invented the wheeled vehicle he became aware of its special requirements. Yet for many centuries the bulk of long-distance traffic was carried by pack-animals travelling over long winding tracks of easy gradients, and the artificial roadways were confined to short routes.

For trade carried by caravans of pack-horses, mules or camels a beaten track was adequate, but as large political units became established the road began to find new uses. Here we come to the second determining factor in the history of overland transport. Not only the type of traffic but also the function of the road itself shaped its developments.

For the purposes of empire, roads were needed not only for the ex-pansion of trade and hence of wealth but also for the movement of armies and, above all, for the transfer of information. In the age of the railway and telecommunications it is easy and natural to forget the fact that until the 1830s information, news, orders to the local administration from the central government and communication of all kinds had to be carried by messenger travelling on horseback overland or more rarely by sea. From very early times we find imperial governments providing themselves with the most efficient and rapid post service possible. Speeds of up to 100 miles a day were fairly common on a well-maintained post route with relays of horses.

Of all the ancient communications networks that of the Romans was the finest and it remained the most remarkable and extensive road system in the world until the twentieth century. Indeed, in terms of fitness for purpose it has still, perhaps, not been surpassed. Without the roads, the Roman empire in Europe would have been impossible. With such an extensive and well-planned communications network within its frontiers, Rome could bring reinforcements to threatened points with remarkable speed, while the central government could make its authority felt on the outposts of the empire more effectively than any power before it.

The Roman roads were remarkable for their time in another respect: they were available to merchants and civilians unconnected with state business. In the Persian empire, as in many others which established a road system, the few fine roads were reserved exclusively for the use of the royal messengers or the royal armies. The royal road from Sardis on the Aegean Sea to the Persian capital at Susa was largely unmetalled, but even so it was an expensive business to maintain the post-horses along the route and to protect the road and its traffic from the depredations of enemy forces or local brigands. Unauthorised use of the road by heavy vehicles would damage the surface intended only for the flying feet of the royal post-horses or the steady tramp of soldiers, while unscheduled traffic held up the royal messengers. In an autocratic empire it was a simple matter to forbid the use of the road to any save those on official business—the road-planners and local authorities of today might sometimes wish for such powers.

The Roman achievement as road-builders was unique in many ways: in the excellence and durability of their engineering; in the audacity of their designers, who had no hesitation, when occasion demanded it, in laying metalled road across the Alps themselves; and in the sophistication and precision of their surveying methods. The techniques of surveying had been known to the ancient Egyptians, like so many other practical and engineering skills. It probably arose from the need to re-establish boundaries and markers of fields and farms when the waters of the Nile receded after the annual flood. But the Egyptians did little for road-building, and it was only with the Romans that the art of land-measurement was applied to the problem of finding the shortest feasible route between two points. Roman techniques and methods are dealt with at length in a later chapter: here we need only notice that in some cases even the Romans were content to follow the routes of their predecessors.

There seems little doubt that the line of Watling Street, which became one of the main roads in Roman Britain, was one of the ancient neolithic ways of the island. Such adaptation was entirely in keeping with Roman practical genius. The age of the route was of no interest but if it offered the best line it would be used. This particular line, like stretches of so many other Roman roads, is still in use today, having been built over to constitute one of the main trunk routes of England. There are equally surprising examples of the persistence of well-chosen routes in America, where some of the most modern highways are built on the alignment of earlier turnpike roads which in their turn followed the course of Indian tracks.

Roman roads had been open to all kinds of traffic but their primary purpose had been military and administrative. Not until our own century was Europe to witness such a thorough and professional approach to road engineering. But land travel was extensive during the Middle Ages. Trade routes were developed, the great pilgrimage routes were opened up and increasingly the highways of Europe were enlivened by the rich and colourful progresses of royal and ducal embassies. The great banking houses established regular courier services and in the fifteenth century King Louis XI of France commanded a post system which enabled him, in times of emergency, to dispatch messages from Tours, in the centre of his kingdom, to its farthest frontiers within twenty-four hours. Yet road-building as such was, and for centuries remained, a matter of piecemeal repairs. There were exceptions such as in the France of Louis XIV, the military roads built in Scotland to service the armies of the Hanoverian kings of England and the military roads built by Napoleon. Any major road-building operation has always been financed by the central exchequer.

Since it is the character of roads to connect places distant from one another and at the same time to serve many smaller intermediary places, there are plenty of possible sources of money—too many in fact, and the disputes between them usually ensured that nothing was done. The toll roads of the eighteenth century went some way to improving the upkeep of certain selected stretches of road but it was obviously not the way to finance an improved national transport system. In rare instances, the central government did take upon itself the financing of major roadworks —usually when there was a compelling military reason. The most telling and significant example of all is the autobahn programme in Hitler's Germany. This had in fact been planned in outline three years before the Nazis came to power and was intended, at least in part, to provide public works for the immense body of unemployed. Yet it was not until the advent of a determined and militarist regime, preparing for the first great exercise in motorised warfare, that the programme came to life. As a by-product it also provided the social advantages for which it had been intended. Thanks primarily to the requirements of a state geared to war, Germany had the world's first network of motor expressways and has maintained her lead in Europe ever since.

But the main stimulus to the road-builder in Europe is very different now. Since the 1950s tourism has come to play an increasingly important part in national economies—in Italy, for example, it is the primary source of foreign currency earnings—and in this situation an investment in motor roads is an investment in foreign trade. Consequently, Italy has the second finest road network in Europe after Germany. (Elsewhere only comparatively slow progress is being made.) In most cases of large investment, action is only taken for an assured cash return or an obvious bonus in terms of prestige. The general economies and improvements in efficiency in the whole industrial and economic life of a nation that good roads bring are undoubtedly understood, but the figures, though large, lack the dramatic impact of, say, a supersonic aircraft. There can be no doubt, for example, that if the £250 million, which is the estimated sum that the British taxpayer has spent on the Concorde project, had been diverted to the motorway programme the nation's economy would have derived far greater advantage from the money. But the glamour, and the pressure groups, ensured the misuse of economic resources to build this flying loss leader for the supermarket of technological Britain. By the time all the bills have been paid it seems fairly clear that close on £400 million will have been 'invested' in Britain's share of the project, while the order books are not yet promising to recoup even that money, let alone provide a reasonable return on capital. The same amount added to the current road programme would make possible some 400 miles of new motorways and improvements to existing routes which, in terms of shortened journey times and running expenses, would expand production, start showing returns from the moment each new stretch was opened and yield a solid return over years ahead.

Although the situation is regrettable and silly, it is not new. As we shall see in the following pages, despite their heavy use and valuable services to the community, roads have generally come at the bottom of the list of political priorities. Generations of travellers have become accustomed to inadequate facilities on the journey and deplorable conditions under foot; in Britain, at least, bad roads are part of our national heritage and complaining about them as common and enjoyable, it would seem, as discussing the weather which determines whether they are passable. Even in the second half of the twentieth century, when almost every aspect of living is being found to be out of date, inconvenient and in need of renovation, the roads like most public utilities are sadly under-financed and the motorist regards the slowly growing mileage of motorways more as a bonus than a birthright.

Our story in this book begins with unmade tracks and ends with speculations about the new forms of transport that the future seems to hold in store; things are going to change radically over the next century but during that period routes that are recognisably roads will still be in use, though the vehicles that travel over them will be very different from anything that we now know. Today we are seeing a great revolution in road-planning and design, greater than anything that has been seen since the time of the Romans. It is hoped that in this book the reader will learn not only of the techniques of the builders but also something of the travellers and traffic that their roads were built to serve.

I

Prehistoric and Ancient Routes

BY THE BEGINNING of the second millennium B.C. a number of long-distance ways had become a part of the pattern of life among the isolated communities of Europe. Since most of these were basically self-supporting, the earliest long-distance trade was in luxury items. The vital element tin was one of the first, following the discovery of bronze-working techniques; others included copper, gold, amber and silk. There was also one essential that was a central element of this early barter, namely salt. A vitally necessary ingredient of the human and animal diet, its sources were not equally distributed, and such centres of production as the salt pans on the western coast of France soon did a thriving trade.

It used to be thought that the earliest routes used by men were simply animal tracks, established by migratory movements and by the search for water, but it now seems unlikely that such tracks played any important part in Man's early travels. The requirements of his communities differed fundamentally from those of animals and there are more practical objections. One of the prime examples used to illustrate this 'animal track' theory was the contention that the trails used by the bison of North America had provided the first overland routes for the Indian tribes there and, at a still later date, the paths of the early white hunters. However, F. G. Roe, who made a study of the subject in the 1920s, found no connection between the animal- and man-made routes. Furthermore, it is an observable fact that the paths leading to the water-holes used by animals do not have any permanence; near the hole they are numerous and distinct, but they quickly disperse and peter out in the bush.

The earliest man-made tracks

Probably the earliest tracks or 'roads' made by Man were the paths to their hunting grounds, though these consisted of little more than a series of observed landmarks and man-made route markers. There are plenty of examples of the skill of Indian pathfinders, whose uncanny sensitivity to the slightest distinguishing features of a landscape enabled them to follow trails that to the untrained eye simply were not there. Such examples are to be found in other parts of the world: the guides employed by European travellers in Asia, in the last century, must have depended to a large extent on their careful observation of the changing face of the landscape. In truly arid conditions or dense jungle the early hunters provided artificial 'landmarks', such as bent or broken boughs in the forest, or little stone cairns in open country.

Not only did the neolithic revolution bring about the establishment of settled communities, however; it also produced the domestication of animals. Thus the traffic of these early routes came to include pack-animals (only at a much later date was the wheel invented). It was now much more important to keep the way clear of loose stones or encroaching vegetation. Thus, from learning a sequence of natural landmarks and then setting up his own road signs, Man took his first tentative steps towards the science of road-building, by clearing the way for a new kind of road-user.

When the stones had been shifted, they were used to build lines of cairns or even low walls, which skirted the road and served to mark it more precisely—particularly in sandy terrains where even the comparatively heavy traffic of laden animals would not do much to compact the surface. In damper lands such as ancient Britain the problems were somewhat different—not so much to mark the route as to find routes which would avoid the hazards of marsh and mud. For similar reasons, and also to provide good look-out points to prepare for possible attack, many early settlements were built on high ground, and the roads that came to link them tended to keep to it. These early 'ridgeways', of which examples were also to be found in various parts of continental Europe, tended to follow the most direct line available. Among the most famous were the Icknield Way, the Ridgeway on the Berkshire–Wiltshire Downs, the Fosse Way and Watling Street. It has been suggested that of the last two, the one received its name from the fact that it was skirted on each side by a fosse or ditch, while stretches of the other may have been protected by a wicker or wattle fence. Such fences seem also to have been built along some of the ancient ways in Germany and other parts of Europe. Another early ridgeway worth mentioning here, though not one used by the Romans, is the so-called Pilgrim Way or Harrow Way from

Salisbury Plain to the heart of Kent. This latter became the chief route for pilgrims travelling to the shrine of Thomas à Becket at Canterbury and from this it derived its name.

The earliest made road network to come to light in western Europe, and so probably the world, was uncovered in the peat-filled basin of the Somerset Levels to the west of Glastonbury. Early in 1970, neolithic trackways were discovered that date from about 2500 B.C. They lead to an artificial 'island' in the bog, consisting of a log platform resting on a bed of brushwood anchored by twigs. One of the trackways has been built up in three successive layers and its whole structure shows marked similarities to the much later road in the Pangola swamps in Hungary.

When these ridgeways were forced to descend into the valleys where the ground was wetter and less firm, they tended to widen out to produce the so-called 'hollow ways'. Even at this early date simple forms of bridge, consisting of large stone slabs stretching from bank to bank, or laid across upright pillar supports, were used to carry the road across small streams. Faced by a wide river-crossing, this meant that the road had to be diverted upstream until a ford could be found. Settlements often grew up around these crossing points and some of the historic towns of Europe had their origin as markets or road-houses set up to serve travellers.

The principle of the wheel may have been known in ancient Sumeria as early as 3000 B.C., but it does not seem to have become a regular feature of transport in the north until about 1500 B.C. Even before this time it seems that attempts were made to straighten the routes of the narrow ridgeways, but as vehicles become more common further developments took place. It is possible that the so-called trackways were first opened up for new traffic. Certainly they would have been more suitable than the ridgeways. They kept to lower contours and avoided steep inclines though they generally kept high enough to be sure of moderately dry and well-drained subsoil. Examples of this kind of track have been found in Ethiopia, Zambia and parts of East Africa while a number are known in ancient Britain. Here evidence has been found of true road works. Some sections show clear signs of artificial levelling, the building of embankments and the digging of ditches. It is possible that such roads and travellers on them were protected by forts and encampments at ten- or twelve-mile intervals—the distance of an average day's march.

These are reasonable deductions from the archaeological remains but it is just as likely that the trackways grew up along the line of already existing settlements. Whatever the reason, the coincidence of roads and settlements, often fortified, does present a familiar pattern in early road systems the world over. Still more fascinating food for speculation is provided by the fact that some English trackways run directly through groups of round barrows. One theory, ingenious if perhaps not convincing, suggested that the round barrows were put up as aids to the surveying of the route—but there are less laborious ways of providing sighting markers. Remembering that barrows were the burial monuments of the early inhabitants of Britain and that the Via Appia, Rome's first great road, came to be lined on both sides with the tombs of the great, we are tempted to suggest that this strange occurrence reflects an age-old burial custom, a memory of which was preserved in the practice of the sophisticated civilisation of Rome.

This contention is to some extent supported by the fact that of forty or so long barrows known on Dartmoor twenty-five are linked to trackways by avenues of monolithic free-standing stones. The most remarkable examples are found in Brittany at Carnac, where there are eleven parallel rows eleven hundred yards long. Their function remains a mystery, but it is at least possible that they marked the processional routes for the high religious festivals. (As we shall see in the next chapter, processional routes provided some of the rare examples of paved roads in the ancient empires of the Middle East.)

Before the coming of the Romans most of Europe's roads were unmetalled, though in the great southern empires, the streets of the major cities were often well paved and comparatively well drained. Neither the climatic conditions nor the terrain of India, Assyria and Persia presented problems confronting a northern imperial power, and consequently the long-distance routes were rarely surfaced. But in the rainy climate of the north and the consequent flooding of all but the high-lying routes at many times of the year, the Romans had to build roads if they were to maintain their empire.

Early surfaced roads

But evidence exists of a few surfaced roads in pre-Roman Europe which form an interesting study. As early as the seventeenth century B.C. we find traces of wooden pavements in the 'lake' villages of Switzerland. Built on stilts in the midst of true lakes or peat bogs, these villages made use of the unfavourable terrain to provide themselves with an ideal form of natural defence. Access by one or two narrow paths ensured that any attacker must either follow an approach well covered by the defenders, or flounder in the surrounding treacherous quagmire. Within the village itself, of course, the same unstable subsoil made journeys between the various buildings hazardous. To meet this villagers built these various types of wooden pavements that, in effect, floated on the peat bog.

To the north of Switzerland there was a vast stretch of loess soil and peat bog above a sandy subsoil, stretching from the Low Countries to the heart of the Ukraine through modern Germany and Poland, and in these conditions a similar solution to the problem of a stable and safe road surface was found. Log or 'corduroy' roads, which date from various periods—some having been built by the Romans—were well adapted to the country over which they ran. A typical example is the Valthersbrug in southern Holland. It is about seven miles long and was made on a bed of loose branches. Above these were laid girders of beech, fir and alder about 4–6 inches thick, running in the direction of the road; above these again came cross-pieces or 'sleepers' of fir, about 3 inches thick. The width of the road varied between 9 and 10 feet and it rested on the peat at a height of about 3 feet above the level of the sandy subsoil. Usually the work was roughly finished, though at the somewhat shorter 'bridge' of Emmer Compascuum the logs and planks were cleanly worked with axe and adze. During the nineteenth century a fierce dispute raged as to the date of these log roads. Some suggested that they were Roman or even later but geological studies of the loess and bog indicated that a large number of them must have been constructed prior to 1500 B.C. The Romans did, however, adapt this local technique to their own purposes, calling such roads '*pontes longi*'. The term correctly sums up the ambivalent character of these floating roads/bridges, built only when the terrain, essentially boggy and dangerous, was too treacherous to carry the weight of the traffic.

The best example of Roman construction on these principles is probably the log road discovered at Brock-Sittard, also in southern Holland. There are also clear indications that the Roman armies used log roads on the frontier with Germany, and beyond it, for their all-important patrol roads. The Romans did not attempt to impose their own well-founded roads on a surface that could not bear them—rather they adapted and perfected existing techniques. Such roads were also durable: royal edicts ordering their repair have survived from the Carolingian period of the ninth century. The technique itself, so reminiscent of that used by Robert Stephenson to carry the railway across Chat Moss in nineteenth-century England, was even longer-lived.

A traveller in eastern Europe in the tenth century noted a 'long bridge' carrying the road in the environs of Prague and a similar feature, more than a mile and a half long, between Magdeburg and Schwerin in eastern Germany. It was about this time that the 'long bridge' or log road over the Pamgola swamps in Hungary must have been built. This is one of the most elaborate examples of medieval road-building to have come to light (it was discovered in 1933). The foundation consisted of a stratum of osiers and twigs secured at intervals with pegs; above this came three levels of logs compacted with twigs; and above this the road surface, about ten feet wide, formed of compacted beaten clay. It is possible that the earlier log roads described above were surfaced with a similar 'pavement' and we know that many of them included the use of pegs to prevent the logs from shifting under the movement of the traffic. Yet despite its seemingly impressive structure, we may question whether it was well built. The success of the log road as such derived from the fact that it was really a floating bridge, distributing the weight of the traffic over the yielding surface of the bog. The earlier examples usually consisted of a raft of twigs and boughs with a single road surface resting on them; the aim in other words was to spread the weight. With the Pamgola road the builders may well have overloaded their raft-like foundation in their attempt to give it a greater solidity.[1] But the principle of the log road, when correctly understood and applied, was a sensible response to the problems of the dangerous and unreliable ground over which it passed. It is of further interest in being the main example of the made road in Europe before the coming of the Romans.

In summing up this look at Europe's earliest roads, we can observe some general principles. They are the work of rational men seeking the most direct and least hazardous route. But from the first these two requirements were in conflict. The most direct way might lie across a marshland or a deep and broad river; the least hazardous might involve a long detour. Many early routes, in the absence of any science of artificial drainage, followed high contours to avoid the hazards of floods or the discomforts of wet going under foot. Others followed the winding course of a river to save an arduous climb. But soon intrepid merchants challenged the most intimidating obstacles of distance and geography. Along their routes new settlements grew up to provide lodgings for the travellers and, where two or more routes crossed, an entrepôt for the exchange of goods. For when we look at such great arteries of trade in ancient Eurasia as the amber route in the north and west and the legendary silk road to the south and east, we must remember that only very rarely did a single caravan travel the whole distance.

The silk route

By the first century B.C. Chinese silk was a common commodity among the rich courtiers of the Persian empire. On the long and arduous road from Susa to Chang-an there were numerous staging posts and flourishing

---

[1] Curiously, the same failure to understand fundamental principles was to be found in eighteenth-century Europe. Then 'engineers' were inclined to build roads on a foundation of loose stones, often as much as three feet deep, which, without adequate draining ditches, provided an ideal catchment trough for rainfall so that the road above was, for large parts of the year, completely waterlogged.

towns. The caravans operated what amounted to a shuttle service, exchanging their gold or valuable horses for the silk of their eastern colleagues and returning to their base town to receive a new cargo. It was a busy and highly profitable route, and its *raison d'être* was the mysterious fabric which the ancient Chinese had learnt to weave from the cocoons of the silk worm.

The art of silk manufacture may have originated in China as early as the year 2600 B.C. Certainly by the time of Confucius in the sixth century B.C. the cloth was cheap enough for all but the most impoverished to buy. Fables of the time illustrate the theme of ignorant folly with the story of the yokel who exchanged his coat of hempen cloth for a silk one. Confucius himself confounded ancient practice when, in one of his dialogues on correct etiquette, he advised that headgear should be woven from silk instead of hemp. (A later commentator noted the reason for this admonition—silk was cheaper and therefore less ostentatious.)

The Chinese were aware of the value of silk in the outside world and kept its manufacture a close secret for more than three thousand years. Major trading contacts to Europe did not begin until the late second and early first century B.C., and they originated after embassies sent by the reigning Han emperor eventually established relations with the court of Persia. The first ambassador to venture into the western lands of the barbarians was Cheng-ch'ien, dispatched by the emperor in about 120 B.C. to arrange a military alliance against the Huns. The allies were to be the Yueh-chih, a confederation of Hunnic tribes occupying a large territory in the southern part of modern Russia, bounded on the north by the Aral Sea, and on the west and east by the Amu-Darya and Syr-Darya rivers. After an incredible journey, in which he reputedly covered some 3,600 miles and suffered ten years' detention by the Huns, Cheng-ch'ien finally reached his destination. He failed to win the alliance he was seeking but on his way he had passed through the land of Kokand where he had been astonished by the sight of some magnificent horses. The Han empire had great need of fine war-horses, the Chinese breed being small, and these animals were to become a major article of trade between China and this distant land on the western boundaries of Tibet. Cheng-ch'ien eventually arrived back in China, after another period of imprisonment by the Huns, and was rightly loaded with honours for what had been an astonishingly bold undertaking in hitherto unexplored territory.

While Cheng-ch'ien was still lost in the unknown lands of central Asia another embassy was sent out to see whether contact could be made with the Persian court. The outcome was successful and from this developed the trade in silk that was to become a means of regular communication between the two empires. The final stage in the silk road came when the Roman conquest of Syria gave them access to the world of the Orient and its luxuries. The shimmering subtle fabric rapidly won such a vogue that in the reign of the Emperor Augustus edicts had to be issued to restrain its use by men, since this was considered effeminate.

Yet although the two greatest capitals in the world, Rome and Chang-an, remained virtually unknown to each other, between them lay the great road along which the merchants made their way. There were in fact two routes: one to the north of the Black Sea and the Caspian, whence it travelled along the southern fringes of the central Asian steppes to the Yellow river; the other to the south, originating in the ports on the seaboard of Syria. This was much the more important of the two and remained so despite attempts by western merchants to find a way to the source of their silk which would enable them to evade the duties and taxes imposed by the Persians.

From Antioch, one of the great cities of the ancient world, the merchant caravans struck out towards the eastern deserts for Palmyra, almost the mid-point between the Mediterranean and the borders of Roman Syria. Soon after it had entered the territories of Persia the road split: one arm headed southward through Seleucia to the head of the Persian Gulf, whence newly opened sea routes took the traveller to the western coast of India; the other arm strode north, across the upper waters of the Euphrates and the Tigris to Ecbatana (now Hamadan). From here the road turned to the north-east, skirting the southern tip of the Caspian Sea and making, by way of three great oases, for Bactra, now called Balkh, the capital of the modern province of Bactria in Afghanistan. From this great entrepôt the road fanned out; one route led north to Samarkand, but the silk route followed its eastward way, running through the lands of the Kushan empire and Sogdiana, over the Pamir mountains.

The empire of the Kushans spread over the whole of modern Afghanistan, Kashmir, the Indus basin, the Punjab and parts of the Tarim desert. In the Persian empire the caravans on this great artery of trade were those of Persian merchants, but from Bactra the traffic was in the hands of Kushans. At the 'Stone Tower', modern Yarkand, the route again forked on the last stretch of its journey to the frontiers of China. One road skirted the north of the Tarim basin, passing through a string of oases; the other proceeded through Khotan. They met at Lop Nor. From this eastern point of the Tarim basin the silk road traversed the still more ancient jade route, along which Chinese convoys had for centuries been carrying the precious stone hewn from the quarries of Tarim. From this long, often devious, but always busy east–west artery other routes penetrated north, to Samarkand, for example, and south, through the Khyber pass to Taxila, near the frontier of the ancient kingdom of Gandara, and still farther south into India.

This network of routes brought not only silk and, much later, porcelain from China but also hides, furs, precious woods, diaphanous muslin cloth and above all ivory, from India. It has been suggested that these routes were known and used even in neolithic times when they would have linked the growing centres of the new agricultural civilisations in the Near East with the settlements later to be amalgamated into the great Chinese empire. Possibly by this same route the secrets of writing and of the wheel were brought to China from the great early civilisations of Mesopotamia. Certainly there had been contact for centuries but it was only with the rise of the Persian and Roman empires that the commerce from east to west reached its height.

We can well imagine the hubbub and bustle of the great trading cities such as Bactra or Kandahar, as the merchants and drivers of different nations unloaded their packs and their masters haggled over the value of their goods. In the earlier centuries the basic means of transport would have been pack animals, such as camels and horses; over some stretches through high and treacherous mountains they remained the only possible means. But later, ox-carts and even horse-drawn carts would have been used, and whatever the means of transport the pattern of travel remained much the same throughout the centuries, even up to recent times.

Over such a vast distance, of course, the weather conditions varied dramatically: from bitter winds and driving snow to the torrid heat of the desert sands. At times the caravan travelled by night to avoid the blazing sun. Often, the road, at its best only a well-beaten track, was lost entirely, and skilled guides, used to navigating by the stars, had to be engaged. A day's march, never less than seven hours, might sometimes be as long as twelve. In addition, the merchants could expect attacks by bandits, unless they took long detours to keep within the protection of the rulers of the various empires and kingdoms through which they passed.

After the day's march, which could rarely have exceeded twenty miles, camp would be made. Each night the animals would have to be unloaded of their burdens; each morning they would be reloaded. If wagons were used they would be arranged to form a laager; here, when sentries had been posted, a fire would be lit and the travellers would settle down to the evening meal. Over the worst of the desert stretches food, water and fuel would have to be carried and any unexpected delays could spell disaster to the whole expedition. Yet century after century trade continued and the profits of a successful mission were enough to keep the merchant eager to undertake his next.

For, as with most of Man's tougher exploits, the incentive had little to do with an abstract love of adventure or a thirst for knowledge. The geographers of the time, striving to assemble by slow degrees an accurate picture of the world, have left many complaints of the bull-headed, single-minded trader who brought back no insight into the many countries he visited. Nor need we be surprised at the fact that, although east and west were in touch with each other over countless generations, they remained almost totally ignorant both of their respective societies and even of their exact whereabouts. Making such journeys and ensuring that they yielded sufficient profit was enough to tax the energies of most men and left little time for the study of unfamiliar political or religious systems. In addition, since any given merchant would normally traverse and re-traverse but one section of the route, the long-distance transmission of news or information produced only the most garbled results.

2

Roads in the Ancient Empires

THE EARLY ROADS so far described were long-distance trade routes which grew up by a natural process. The roads of the empire builders, however, were laid out artificially and were often elaborately maintained to serve the purposes of war and administration. Such roads tended to work on the lands through which they were built, breeding communities which had no other *raison d'être* but the road itself.

India

One of the most interesting of ancient civilisations was that of the Indus valley. Unsuspected until its discovery in 1922, it seems to have arisen towards the beginning of the third millennium B.C., and was overthrown by the incursion of Indo-European barbarians, the ancestors of subsequent Indian and European civilisations. Though the culture of Harappa and Mohenjo-Daro, the great cities of the Indus valley, seems to have been in decline even before the invasion of the northerners, at its height it was clearly a great civilisation. The remains of the cities revealed brick-paved streets; under-street drainage, with channels running from the house into covered sewers in the centre of the streets; and curved street corners that clearly suggest the use of wheeled traffic and the understanding of the effects of heavy vehicles turning in a confined space. After the invasion of the Indo-Europeans, this part of India was in a parlous state for some centuries. But by the ninth century B.C. the work of the conquerors had raised a new civilisation which in its turn understood the value of well-paved streets. The surface was produced by laying a level of mixed clay and broken pottery that was then fused by being burnt *in situ* on the sur-face of the road.

The next great period of Indian civilisation was that of the Mauryan rulers, the chief among them being Chandragupta and Asoka, from the fourth to the second centuries B.C. Greek writers testify to the high level achieved and there are some interesting references to the roads built and used in the north and north-west of India during this period. From these Greek commentaries, and from others by Indian writers, a number of significant points emerge. It is apparent, for example, that the Mauryan empire understood as fully as the Romans the need for efficient communi-cation. There was actually an officer of state charged with the oversight of the highways. His job was to keep them free of obstructions, to maintain bridges in good repair and to see to the upkeep of those rare stretches of road that were paved; another vital function was the erection of mile posts marking the distances along the road and indicating the destinations of the various side roads. In addition to these there were official registers of the stages of the main arterial route. This was the royal road running from west to east through the imperial capital of Pataliputra (modern Patna), from which 'itineraries' or route guide-books were drawn up for important travellers. Making use of this kind of record, the Greek philosopher Eratosthenes (who, incidentally, also estimated the circumference of the earth with some accuracy) was able to estimate the length of this great road as something in the region of 10,000 Greek *stadia* from the western frontier to the capital, and a further 6,000 *stadia* from there eastwards. In total this represented a length of about 2,600 miles, and throughout the whole distance the road seems to have been well equipped with staging posts and guard-houses so that the post of the great Indian rulers of the period must have been capable of an average speed of something like 100 miles a day.

Although the most important road of the empire, this was not the only one. Strabo, another Greek, writing in the first century A.D., refers to three roads running southwards from Bactria to India. These would certainly have been less thoroughly guarded and maintained since they were used largely for trade: the riches of India were sent up to the great emporium of Balkh, then westwards to the markets of Syria and to the Mediterranean world. But in general the roads of this great empire were carefully super-vised and, wherever possible, as carefully maintained. Different words were used for roads of varying widths and hence of varying functions. One contemporary source gives details of the drainage facilities of the city streets; another refers to the obligation of the regions through which the main roads passed to build rest-houses and hostelries for travellers and garrisons for the forces detailed to protect the road. It also mentions penalties for the pilfering of building materials. Although outside the cities few sections of the roads were paved, within them various paving materials were used, including fired brick, stone slabs, a form of cement-bound surface and gravel.

Perhaps the most interesting road of which we have record from this great period of ancient Indian history is that of the processional way around the Dharmarajika *stupa* at Taxila. It was made from a lime-and-sand mortar in which were set fragments of different-coloured shells arranged in geometrical patterns. This elaborate and decorative type of pavement is strongly reminiscent of those built for the sanctuaries of ancient Assyria and Egypt.

Ancient Mesopotamia and Egypt

Despite the most recent archaeological discoveries the region centred upon the valleys of the Euphrates and Tigris remains one of the most important and earliest hubs of the city civilisations. Little is known about the roads of the earliest of all, that of Sumer, though we know from the magnificent grave furniture of Ur that wheeled vehicles were used. A record from the reign of the greatest king of Babylonia, Hammurabi (*c.* 1750 B.C.), shows that the ruler expected even his great officials to be able to cover the distance between Larsa and Babylon the capital, a distance of more than 125 miles, in less than forty-eight hours. We have a little more information about the great successor civilisation of the Assyrians and perhaps the earliest recorded road engineers are the '*ummani*' or pioneer corps of the army of Tiglath Pileser I (*c.* 1100 B.C.) whose scribes have left a vivid description of their work in making a road through the mountain ranges to the north of Mesopotamia as the king pursued his enemies. Under one of Tiglath Pileser's successors, Sargon II (*c.* 750 B.C.), we hear of watch-houses built along a route at a distance of two hours' travel, written itineraries for the use of travellers, and the building of a paved road of polygonal limestone slabs from the royal palace near Nineveh to the banks of the Tigris.

Especially interesting are the ceremonial ways recorded in the Assyrian empire from the tenth century B.C. onwards. During this period too the paving of city streets, either with stone or gravel, became more frequent. The most remarkable example of city road-building, however, is probably the road of the kings at Nineveh, built in the reign of Sanherib (*c.* 700 B.C.). This impressive processional way was about ninety feet wide, well paved and lined down its entire length by lofty pillars designed to mark its boundaries to all men. To make doubly sure that his splendid highway lost none of its grandeur by the encroachments of private development, Sanherib invoked the kind of sanction that many a local planning authority today must often dream of. Anyone building even a balcony overhanging the royal highway was liable to suffer the extreme penalty by impalement on the finials of his own roof.

Neither the climate, nor the terrain, nor the comparatively late arrival of the wheel encouraged the building of engineered roads in the legendary civilisation of Egypt. Here, as in so many parts of the ancient world, the main business was making the roadway accessible—clearing loose stones, building protective and marking walls, digging wells and providing rest- and guard-houses. Among the most impressive 'roads' built by the Egyptians were the immense causeways constructed during the building of the Pyramids for the supply of the building blocks used to raise the massive structures. Another interesting example is the elaborate system of roads built around the capital of the boldly heretical Ikhnaten at Tel el Amarna. What appear to be patrol roads skirt the perimeter, as if of a beleaguered garrison, and seem to emphasise the degree to which the Pharaoh's unorthodox religious opinions, which led him to attempt to abolish all Egypt's ancient gods, had isolated him from the affections of his people. A still more interesting though equally short stretch of roadway is the stone-paved ceremonial route linking the temples of Bast and Thoth at the holy city of Bubastis. Nearly half a mile long and some 400 feet wide, it ran straight through the market-place of the town and was lined on either side with lofty trees. Another road, that built for the Pharaoh Rameses III at his new city of Perrameses, was described by a visitor as a holy road glistening with flowers.

Processional ways

It is perhaps worth pausing to consider the purposes and nature of these ceremonial ways in the ancient world. Obviously the road of the gods had to be more splendid and more magnificent than anything used by mortals, but this splendour had to be reflected not only in the decorations and beautiful trees planted alongside the route, or in the inlay of coloured marble and shells in the surface, but also in the quality of the engineer-ing. During the great religious processions, the chariots, arks and statues of the gods themselves were carried and rolled along with great pomp and ceremony. And when the gods were moved the greatest precautions had to be taken; in India anyone unfortunate enough to slip before the wheels of the sacred chariot or juggernaut would be crushed to death to avoid any delay in the god's progress. Even in the more familiar world of the Old Testament we find that when the wagon carrying the Ark of the Lord was jolted one of the bearers who attempted to steady it was struck dead by the angry god. Given these kind of beliefs the peoples of the ancient world naturally took all possible care to ensure that the road over which the god would travel, no matter how short, was as smooth and secure as possible.

The finest surviving Assyrian processional ways were found at the temple of Ishtar in Assur and at Babylon. Both are considerable works; at Assur the road was laid on a foundation of burnt bricks, the pavement being made from rock slabs in which artificial wheel ruts had been carved to receive the wheels of the holy chariot—another precaution to ensure the smooth procession of the god. At Babylon the ceremonial road, called Aiburshabu, had a total length of 1,800 yards; at the Ishtar gate it rose to a height of forty feet above the town and must have formed an awe-inspiring spectacle when in use.

Persia

Towards the end of the seventh century B.C. the power of the Assyrians was broken by the growing might of the Medes on their northern and eastern frontiers. The triumph of the latter was short-lived, however; by the year 500 B.C. they had been utterly displaced by their former allies the Persians who, under a succession of great rulers, extended their power throughout the area represented by modern Iran, Syria, Turkey and Iraq, pushed their frontiers to the Mediterranean seaboard and conquered Upper Egypt. Although it did not maintain these extended boundaries, and indeed suffered severe vicissitudes of fortune, the Persian empire was to last a thousand years, remaining one of the two great powers of the ancient world. Its road system, while extensive, did not represent the same kind of engineering achievement as that of Rome. There were few paved roads, though the Greek historian Diodorus, writing in the first century B.C., does refer to a paved road between Susa and Ecbatana, a distance of more than 200 miles. Nevertheless the Persian kings, like all the great imperial rulers of the ancient world, were able to rely on the best and fastest communications system that money could provide. We know, for example, that the distance between Susa and Babylon could be covered in less than two days, representing a speed of nearly 100 miles a day; while on the famous royal road from Ephesus on the Mediterranean, through Sardis, to Susa the royal capital, a distance of over 1,600 miles, a messenger could cover the whole distance in nine days. Such speeds were possible because of numerous staging posts, each of which maintained a sizeable stable.

Roads of the Inca empire

The greatest empire of ancient America, that of the Inca, stretched for more than 3,000 miles down the Pacific coast from Quito in Ecuador to the

centre of modern Chile. Geographically it comprised three distinct regions: the Andean highlands; a jungle strip to the west; and farther to the
west a desert coastal strip. In 1527 this vast and strictly ordered domain
was turned topsy turvy by the audacity (and unexpected weaponry) of a
body of Spanish marauders numbering not more than two hundred.
Fierce and effective resistance was maintained for forty-five years but it
finally succumbed to Christian deceit and violence. The European de-
stroyers, however, soon learnt to respect the efficient and well-ordered
state that they had overrun.

The people ruled by the Inca—the name of the ruler himself—were not
a motley of slaves and tribes; nor was the conquering nation the first to
found a high culture in the region. The ancestors of the Inca emperors
settled in the valley of Cuzco, in the southern part of modern Peru, during
the twelfth century, and by slow but sure conquest came to extend their
sway over a vast coastal empire of some 350,000 square miles. The basis of
their success was invincible ruthlessness in war and a native talent for
administration in peace. The achievement is the more remarkable since it
was the work of a people without a developed system of writing, so important to the administration of the empires of the Old World. Yet the
Inca did have one vital thing in common with the Romans, the Persians
and the Assyrians: an extensive and ever-growing system of roads. These
were the highways of conquest and the arteries of empire, and they were
planned from the first, or so the archaeological evidence implies, according to a uniform design.

The pattern of Inca roads, extensive and impressive as it is, is nevertheless essentially simple. The system was like a rope ladder along the length
of the empire: the supports were, east, the royal road along the heights
of the Andes and, west, the coastal road; the rungs were roads running
down the main valleys from the interior to the sea. From this main military and administrative network branched other routes including those
to the gold mines, but essentially the system operated in the service
of the Inca and his government. Once again we see how a great road
system of the past depended in the last resort on the ambitions of
empire.

The royal road, which stretched for a distance of some 3,250 miles, has
been described as the longest trunk road in the world prior to the nineteenth century; the coastal road too could be considered impressive, even
though it was 1,000 miles shorter. The traffic using these two great highways and their cross-links was almost entirely pedestrian. In common with
the other American Pre-Columbian civilisations the Incas did not de-
velop wheeled vehicles.[1] The only beast of burden, the sure-footed llama,

[1] They seem to have been entirely ignorant of the principle of the wheel, not even
using it for children's toys, like the Aztecs.

made no heavier demands on a route than did a man. Inca roads, therefore, were almost entirely unpaved.

The engineering talents of this ancient people, so astonishingly revealed in their vast and unmortared masonry, were fully exploited in the survey-ing and construction of their roads. The steep ascents and descents, un-avoidable in this, one of the most mountainous countries in the world, were negotiated by long stairways which reach up sometimes for hundreds of feet. Clinging to the precipitous sides of deep gorges, springing across rocky and raging torrents hundreds of feet below, or stretching for mile upon mile across high arid plateaux often more than 15,000 feet above sea level, these roads provided speedy passage for the mighty armies and fleet-footed royal messengers for which they had been built. Although the only paved surfaces were at the approaches to important towns or at stretches liable to flooding, the term 'built' is the correct one. It has been shown, for example, that throughout the whole of its 2,500 miles the coast road maintained a basic width of twenty-four feet, departing from it only under the most difficult conditions. Causeways were built and cliffs cut away to keep to this standard gauge, while, as on the great royal highway, retaining walls skirted either side, both to define the road and to hold back drifting sand and occasional flood-waters. For the Inca engineers, like all serious road-builders, fully appreciated the need for effective drainage. As far as possible they carried their highway along contours well above water-courses and rivers, but where passage of low-lying or marshy terrain was unavoidable either drains and culverts were provided or the road itself was raised on a causeway—one of these works extending for no less than eight miles.

Given the nature of the terrain it was inevitable that bridges would be needed to cross the small turbulent rivers and deep narrow ravines. Thousands were in fact built, and some were still being used in the nine-teenth century. Without knowledge of the keystone arch the Inca engineer fell back on the primitive yet effective technique of the cantilevered or corbelled arch, with which distances of up to about thirty feet could be spanned. In this method the bridge is constructed out of large slabs of stone piled one above the other, each one projecting a little farther than the one below. The bridge floor is provided by a single long slab strong enough to carry the required weight over the now much reduced gap.

The most breathtaking of all Inca works, however, was the rope bridge, of which the most famous, that of San Luis Rey, was in operation well into the nineteenth century. The first bridge over this fantastic gorge, carved out of the Andes by the Apurimac river had been constructed in the middle of the fourteenth century. It spanned a distance of 150 feet at a height of some 300 feet above the river. The approach on one side was up a precipitous cliff; the road here was little more than an eighteen-foot-wide ledge. On the other side of the river the road continued its upward ascent across the broad face of the mountain range. The break in the road was crossed by a structure of almost fairy-like daring that terrified the wits out of the Spaniards when they first saw it. It was a rope suspension structure and had neither stay- nor guy-ropes to steady it in the gales that drove from time to time down the canyon. Yet so long as the cables were renewed at frequent intervals it was quite strong enough to take the traffic for which it was designed; it was so high above the river that it was clear of any danger from flooding, and while it might sway frighteningly in the wind it was too flexible to snap. The two suspension cables, which were slung over the tops of stone towers at either end, were massive spun ropes as thick as a man and some 200 feet in length, about twenty feet being buried in the ground on each side of the gorge. Beneath them, and attached to them by thinner ropes spaced about every two feet, was the floor of the bridge, which consisted of wooden slats laid across another three stout cables. And that was all. No wonder the European eye, used to the heavy squat appearance of medieval strong bridges, was appalled! Yet such suspension bridges, of which the one described was undoubtedly the finest, served the Inca road-builders and their Spanish successors for half a millennium.

The building of the bridge of San Luis Rey marked the first dramatic step out of the Inca's base territory, and it was followed everywhere by the roads. In the end armies could be delivered at speed to threatened frontiers, could put down rebellion at any point in the empire—and news of rebellion travelled just as quickly to the great Inca in his capital. The horse was unknown, and the magnificent network of roads provided what amounted to a veritable running track for the royal messengers. Along the whole length were staging posts, about a mile and a half apart, each housing a small garrison and a relay of professional runners. Each stage was sufficiently short for a rapid relay and, operating day and night, the service could carry a message from the capital at Cuzco to the city of Quito, 1,250 miles away, in a matter of five days. This meant averaging ten miles per hour along a road never less than 15,000 feet above sea level—a speed never achieved by the regular Roman imperial post!

3

Roman Roads in Italy

THE HISTORY OF Rome's roads begins in the year 312 B.C. when the Censor, Appius Claudius, persuaded the senate to construct a road from Rome to Capua, 130 miles to the south. Capua had been recently captured from the Samnites and controlled the rich and prosperous district of Campania with its important coastal salt pans. As we have seen, this commodity was a vital one in ancient times, and Rome was determined not to lose its hard-won access. Thus the road was functional from a trading as well as a military standpoint, a principle that was to be followed wherever possible in the Roman road system.

From this remarkable beginning the system spread throughout Europe, North Africa and the Middle East until it reached a total estimated length of 53,000 miles. It is important to stress that, despite the legendary prestige of the Romans as road-builders, by no means all of these miles of road were favoured with carefully engineered and well-laid surfaces. Many of the lesser roads throughout the empire were simply well-maintained earth tracks, while even the major routes were not built to a standard pattern; the techniques of construction varying with the terrain. But one thing all these roads had in common was reliability. Where building methods differed from the standards of the Italian roads, it was to accommodate regional differences of soil or climate or, occasionally, of function. It was possible to travel from York to Constantinople and on to Jerusalem, using good roads all the way. With a fast courier the journey could probably have been made in six weeks—a journey time that was not to be bettered until the coming of the railways. During this period the means of transport remained virtually unchanged, and for many centuries the use of vehicles was much more restricted than it had been under Rome.

The Via Appia and the South

In pre-Roman Italy the Etruscans, who had based their power in the Po valley to the north of Rome and had used the wheeled war-chariot, had laid out fairly extensive, if primitively engineered, routes, as had the Carthaginians. It was perhaps from them that the Romans derived the idea of the constructed road designed for wheel traffic. But the Via Appia, which at first stretched only from Rome to Capua, was so different from anything that went before that it is pointless to try to trace its origins to any source more abstruse than the native Roman aptitude for adaptation and thoroughness, touched in this case with a liberal degree of sheer and brilliant invention. This road was remarkable not only for its completeness as an engineering achievement but also for being the first stretch of paved road of any length in the history of Western man.

The Via Appia remained one of the main arteries of the road system in Italy, but had other remarkable characteristics. For over 100 miles on its route southwards from the imperial city it was lined with the tombs of generations of famous Romans (*see* Plate 2). This strange yet fashionable cemetery was inaugurated, so to speak, by the builder of the road himself whose family erected a magnificent tomb for him just outside the city. Thereafter more and more impressive monuments were built; decorated with marble effigies and inscriptions in the superb characters of monumental Roman lettering they became one of the sights of the empire and side-walks had to be provided to accommodate the many strollers and pedestrians on this somewhat macabre sight-seeing tour. Indeed, the funerals themselves which brought the V.I.P.s to their final resting place must have been a still more impressive sight. Usually at night, the processions of pall-bearers, mourners and torch-carriers slowly made their way down the magnificent road. Arrived at the new mausoleum, the cortège halted and the body was placed on the pyre prepared for it. At a signal a flame leapt up into the dark Italian night and the body was consumed in a brilliant tableau of colour; when the fire had died down, the ashes, from which the soul of the departed had flown up to the stars, were gathered up in an urn and placed in the marble tomb.

From Capua the Via Appia was continued during the following centuries east across the southern ranges of the Apennines to the port of Brundisium (modern Brindisi) on the coast of the heel of Italy. About six miles to the south of Capua, the Via Popilia forked to the south and ran down to Salerno on the coast; from there it went inland through Lucania and Brutium (the toe of Italy), joining the coast about seventy-five miles above its terminal point in Reggio. The Via Appia itself struck north-east to Benevento, then eastwards through the province of Samnium and the southern part of Apulia to Taranto, on the 'inside' coast of Calabria (the

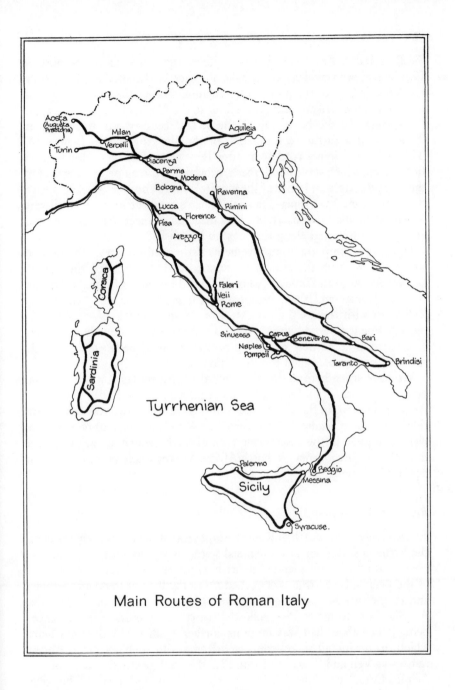

Main Routes of Roman Italy

'heel' of Italy). From here it struck across the peninsula to the port of
Brindisi, where travellers could take ship across the southern stretch of
the Adriatic Sea for the port of Dyrrachium, whence the superb road ran
on through the Balkans and Asia Minor to the Mesopotamian frontiers of
the empire. At the beginning of the second century A.D. the Emperor
Trajan built a further continuation of the Via Appia from Benevento.
This left the original road soon after Benevento, but the milestones on
this stretch, which served both roads, proclaimed the emperor's regard for
the great Republican father of the empire's roads and were inscribed with
the route name Via Appia-Traiana. Trajan's road then struck north-east
to central Apulia, went down in a long diagonal to meet the Adriatic road
at Bari, and followed along the coast to Brindisi.

Of the other important improvements to the road system south of Rome
we should mention the stretch of coast road that continued the line of
the Via Appia from Sinuessa (where it turned inland for Capua) down the
coast to Naples and then, proceeding still southwards along the coast,
joined up with the southward extension of the Appian Way about ten
miles before it entered Salerno. Naples was also linked directly to Capua,
a distance of some fifty miles, by a smaller but equally efficient road,
still well preserved, called the Via Campana.

We have space here to describe only the main routes that the Romans
opened up in their six hundred years of mastery in the Italian peninsula.
As we have seen, in the south these routes gave access over the sea on one
side to the great roads of the eastern part of the empire, and on the other
were continued in the coastal ring road of Sicily, which led in turn, by a
much longer sea journey, to north Africa. Yet the roads in the north were
equally important.

Roads of the North

Immediately to the north of Rome was the land of the city's ancient rulers,
the Etruscans. Reduced to provincial status by its vigorous young neighbour, Etruria was still a land of flourishing towns. Like every other region
of the peninsula, Etruria was opened up to the flow of trade and armies,
and to the processes of administration, by a network of roads. The Via
Aurelia, from Rome to Pisa, followed the coast for most of the distance,
being joined about half-way up in its northerly journey by the Via Clodia
which, by an inland route, connected Rome with such ancient Etruscan
centres as Veii and Tuscana. From Pisa the road, under the name of Via
Aemilia Scauri, continued along the coast to Genoa and then, still hugging
the coast and now known as Via Julia Augusta, passed through modern Nice
on its way to the important ancient seaport of Marseilles in southern Gaul.

Travelling due north, another important road linked Rome with

Arretium and Florence, while to the north-east lay the route of another of the greatest of the ancient roads of Italy, the Via Flaminia. Begun in 264 B.C., within forty years it had reached the town of Spoletum, some eighty miles to the north of the capital and in the very heart of the Apennines. Although Augustus was to improve the route by building bridges two hundred and fifty years later, even within a few years of reaching Spoletum it provided easy access to Rome: it was down the Flaminian Way that Hannibal led his armies to the attack on Rome. Some five hundred years after this the road was at the heart of another great historic confrontation of the ancient world, for it was at the battle of the Milvian bridge, where the Flaminian Way left Rome, that Constantine won the historic fight that was to make him master of the empire. Like all the great roads of Rome, this carried a considerable volume of commercial traffic, and the market of the Milvian bridge was one of the most important in Rome and a favourite resort of citizens of all classes. Like many street markets today it was not simply a place for buying and selling but an ideal one in which to spend an idle hour or so, watching or participating in the haggling, eating well—it was renowned for its roast pork—and, if one happened to be the youthful Nero, shocking the bourgeoisie.

From Spoletum, the Flaminian Way continued northwards through the mountainous country of central Italy, linked on its way by minor roads to such small towns as Assisi, until it reached the Adriatic coast. Here it turned north-west, following the coast to the town of Ariminum (modern Rimini) where it forked, one branch continuing up the coast to the marsh-bound city of Ravenna, the other, called the Via Aemilia, striking still farther to the north-west until it met the Po. This great road ran down the whole length of the ancient province of Aemilia; starting at Ariminum it passed through Bononia (Bologna), Modena and Parma on its way to Placentia (modern Piacenza), an important town in the Po valley and the major road junction to the north of Rome. Here the traveller from the Adriatic would meet merchants and imperial messengers, soldiers and officials converging from north, east and west. The Via Claudia Augusta brought amber, furs and slaves from central Germany, down the valley of the River Adige through Trent to Verona; from there one arm went eastwards to Aquileia at the head of the Adriatic, while the other continued southwards to Verona, and from there south-west through Cremona to Placentia. The traveller might continue his southward journey down the Via Claudia Augusta to the Ligurian coast at Vada Sabatia (modern Savona) and could from there continue into southern Gaul along the coast road. Alternative routes to Gaul were provided by roads to the north of the Po valley, one of which ran due west from Placentia to Turin, later turning south in the Cottian Alps through the Mont Genèvre pass to Brigantio (modern Briançon), then proceeding south-west down the valley of the River Durance. The other road from Placentia to Gaul took a still more northerly route through Augusta Praetoria (modern Aosta) and the Little St Bernard pass, and then turned down the valley of the River Isere.

To the north-west of Placentia lay Mediolanum, modern Milan. Until 222 B.C. it had been the capital of a Gallic tribe, but after its conquest by Rome it was soon linked to the growing road system of northern Italy and became an increasingly important city. From it a road ran eastwards through Bergomum (modern Bergamo), Brixia (Brescia), Verona, Vicentia (Vicenza) to Aquileia. To the west this road continued through Milan to Vercellae (Vercelli), where it joined the route from Placentia to Augusta Praetoria.

Such, then, were some of the main roads of Roman Italy. As was to be expected they continued in use far longer than roads in other parts of the empire. Furthermore, the centuries of Roman civilisation established a pattern of settlement in the peninsula that has remained little changed until the present day. For this reason, and because the Roman routes were not only magnificently surfaced but also expertly surveyed, they still form an integral part of the road system of Italy.

Organisation and construction

Confronted with the achievement of the Romans as road-builders, a writer is bound to find himself fighting off superlatives, and it is doubtful whether any other single monument from Man's past has been of more lasting service than the roads of Italy which, for more than two thousand years, have carried trade and travellers over often difficult terrain with the least possible hardship. Before turning briefly to the engineering of these magnificent highways we should remind ourselves that besides them there were innumerable other roads of lesser quality. There were three broad classifications. First came the *viae publicae,* also called the *viae praetoriae,* owned and maintained by the state; second, there were numerous *viae rusticae* or country roads which were built over comparatively short distances by private individuals or local communities to link small townships with each other or to the nearest main road; finally, there were the *viae vicinales* which were little better than the dirt tracks that had served men for generations. In certain parts of the empire, where terrain and weather permitted, even the best-quality roads were in fact highly finished, levelled earth tracks, termed by the Roman writer Ulpian *viae terrenae*; elsewhere somewhat more elaborate surfaces were laid consisting of heavy gravel on little or no foundation, and called *via glaratae*; finally we come to the solidly paved and well-founded *viae munitae*.

Appius Claudius Crassus had urged that the road to Capua be provided with firm foundations and here lay the chief contribution of Rome to the science of road engineering. From the first, heavy vehicles and a large volume of traffic were allowed for, great care being taken to ensure not only a hard-wearing surface but also good drainage. Initially the ground was levelled, then drainage ditches were dug on either side of the route; next a foundation level of heavy stones was laid; above this came a stratum of broken bricks or pottery. In other examples the road was excavated to a depth of three feet; the trench was filled with loose stones, and above this was laid the surface of well-fitting hexagonal blocks of volcanic stone.

Traffic and travellers

These roads carried a wide variety of traffic and were not simply reserved for the use of the legions or government messengers, though troops were constantly on the move—reinforcing garrisons, putting down insurrections, even taking part in the building of new stretches of road. For although the Romans had large supplies of slave labour to draw on, many miles of road were built by soldiers. Local labour was not always available; in other places the terrain was too hostile for any but the most hardened men, while in times of peace public works were sometimes given to the military as a matter of policy to keep the soldiers from idleness and avoid disciplinary problems.

The heavy volume of wheeled traffic has left its traces in the deep ruts that score some surviving pavements. Although few actual remains of the wheeled vehicles of ancient Rome have survived, we have plenty of evidence of their wide variety from carved reliefs and wall paintings. They ranged from the light racing gig to heavy ceremonial four-wheeled wagons. More common than these was the slow-moving but capacious ox-cart; capable of carrying loads of up to half a ton and drawn by two or four oxen it was used for all bulk transport. There were few passenger vehicles and they were in any case the preserve of the rich. The most magnificent of these *raeda* was the one used by members of the imperial family; a spacious four-wheeled vehicle luxuriously appointed with cushions and drapes and splendidly ornamented within and without, it was drawn by a team of two or four horses driven by postilions. A still larger form of conveyance was called the *carruca*. This could be used for sleeping *en route*, being fitted with bedding and blinds. Such a vehicle was used by the historian Pliny, who, as a government official, travelled extensively around the empire. Nevertheless most of the traffic of ancient Rome was either pedestrian or horse. The greatest feat of speed that the world was to see until the coming of the railways was, hardly surprisingly, achieved over the roads of the empire. It is recorded that Tiberius, later to be emperor, travelled 200 miles in a single day in his furious drive to the bedside of his dying brother Drusus at Lyons. Tiberius travelled by light chariot and with frequent changes of horses maintained such a punishing speed that the vehicle itself had to be replaced three times.

But for most fast travel, and indeed most passenger travel of any kind, the usual mode was horseback. Administrative communications would have been carried by the imperial post. About every ten miles there was a posting station with a stable for up to forty horses; here ostlers and fully trained vets were available, day and night. The central government could rely on an average speed of 100 miles a day for urgent messages, though not infrequently this was bettered, and even speeds of 150 miles per day were achieved. The riders themselves were highly experienced and their equipment was practical—they wore breeches, conventionally considered the barbarian fashion, but for horsemen expected to ride in all weathers very much more comfortable than the standard Roman dress which left the legs bare. They also wore heavy woollen cloaks and, a nice touch, flat 'shovel' hats like the one worn by Mercury, the messenger of the gods.

This elaborate and costly service was maintained exclusively for government use. The ordinary citizen could expect his letters, entrusted to merchants or other travellers as chance offered, to be long-delayed and often lost—either through the attacks of bandits on merchant caravans in the more remote parts of the empire, or, we may imagine, through the sheer carelessness of the carriers. In addition to the staging houses of the emperor's post the main roads of Italy were well served by a number of hostelries, some of which were state-controlled and built out of local taxes while others, somewhat less pretentious and, it appears, a good deal less comfortable, were built and run by private individuals. Yet some of these taverns were of a good standard and earned considerable reputations, much as the better roadhouses do today. In Italy most of the roads had been built to link towns and settlements already existing at fairly short intervals, but in the empire at large they gradually made permanent changes in the lands through which they passed. It often happened that the small settlements that grew up around taverns and hostels gave birth to townships that, in the course of centuries, became great cities.

Administration, survey and maintenance

As the imperial administration declined so the roads gradually fell into disrepair. Despite their fine quality they, like any others, required constant maintenance and to ensure this the government appointed a board of highway curators whose duties also included the supervision of works on new roads. The more important routes were entrusted to the special care of a single curator—some public figure would become curator of the Appian Way and spend much of his own private fortune to improve and maintain this most famous of all Roman roads.

This attention to the administrative requirements of maintenance marks the seriousness with which the Romans took the business of communications. From the earliest years the conquering armies that gradually brought the motley tribes of Italy under the sway of Rome were followed by skilled surveyors and hardy 'navvies' who marked the subjugation of the new territory with the hard white line of a paved highway. These roads soon won, and have ever since enjoyed, a reputation for their undeviating straightness. (An example is the astonishing Via Aemilia which in the 163 miles of its course from Rimini to Piacenza hardly once departed from the straight line.) The Roman surveyor laid out his road in a number of straight sections, taking bearings from one high point on another several miles distant, and then laying down the line for the builders to follow. As the foundations and pavement gradually crept forward, other work gangs went ahead to drain marshy lands or bridge rivers that lay on the route, while skilled masons cut and engraved the milestones. In their most elaborate form these carried the name of the emperor with all his titles, the year of his reign, the name of the route and the distance in miles, either from the Forum in Rome or from the nearest large town. These milestones, like everything built by the Romans, were designed to last, being set in a stone base and inscribed with the handsome monumental lettering that was perhaps one of the greatest artistic achievements of this mighty race of engineers.

The traveller in ancient Italy could be sure not only of a firm well-sign-posted road, provided with wayside inns; he could also, if he wished, study the journey that he proposed to take in advance. The booksellers of the capital stocked numerous road maps or *itinerarii* which indicated the main halting places on the route, the rivers and other geographical features that were relevant and the distances between the main towns and inns. These guides were probably copied from full-scale official maps—we know that such existed, although no originals have survived. However, there is in the Nationalbibliothek at Vienna a remarkable document known as the Peutinger Table. This is a thirteenth-century copy of a map of all the military roads of the empire—the original was probably made in the fourth century A.D. and must certainly have been commissioned by some government department. Thanks to this immensely detailed document our knowledge of the road network of the empire is extremely thorough, even of those places where all trace of the roads themselves has disappeared.

Perhaps the most magnificent road map ever produced, both for its subject and for its workmanship, was the map of the Roman empire which was made for the Emperor Augustus and fixed to the wall of his private bedroom. Made of sheet gold it had the roads marked as engraved lines and the chief towns and cities of the empire picked out with precious stones. But it was not from this beautiful if somewhat ostentatious record of Rome's grandeur that the humble guide-books mentioned above would have been taken. Under the orders of the Emperor Vespasian (A.D. 69–79), a vast map of the empire and its roads, carved out of marble, was set up in the Forum at Rome for all to see and study at their leisure.

From this chapter and the one that follows it is clear that the Romans were not merely road-builders, they were also masters of the whole business of communications. It is for this, as much as the quality of their engineering, that their pre-eminence in the history of European civilisation is assured.

4

Roman Roads in the Empire

WHEN THE PLANNED European network of 'E' roads and the Middle East Highway are complete, they will cover much the same routes as those of the Roman empire. One route took the traveller from the north French coast near Boulogne down to Rheims, then on through Munich, Linz, Vienna and Budapest to Istanbul. From here one road led due east along the southern coast of the Black Sea, while another went over the central uplands of Anatolia, southwards to the Syrian desert, down the valley of the Euphrates, and on to the cities of Mesopotamia and the Persian Gulf. Another important route linked the ports of the North African coast, from Algeria to Alexandria, while all the main centres of Gaul and Spain were served by fine roads, from Cadiz to Paris, from Lyons to Mérida. The distant province of Britain was equally well provided—indeed, its network seems to have been second only to that of Italy itself in its coverage. In this chapter we shall describe the roads in the outlying areas of Spain, Africa and Britain, each of which present points of special interest.

Along the Mediterranean coast the road ran out of Italy from Genoa on to Marseilles; thence it turned northwards towards Nîmes while another road went up the Rhône valley to the important city of Lyons. From Nîmes the road to Spain returned to the coast to skirt the Pyrenees on its way to Barcelona and Tarragona. Two other roads entered Spain, one following the valley of the Garonne to Toulouse and thence striking over the mountains to Saragossa; the other headed south from Bordeaux, skirted the Atlantic coast and crossed near the modern frontier town of Hendaye.

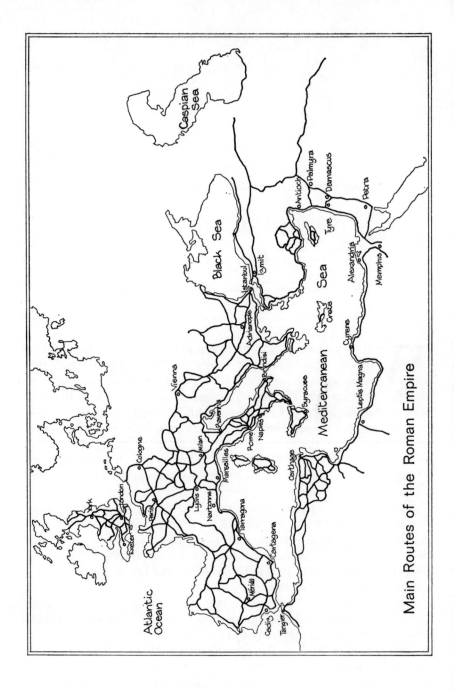

Main Routes of the Roman Empire

Atlantic Ocean

Caspian Sea

Black Sea

Mediterranean Sea

Palmyra
Damascus
Antioch
Petra
Tyre
Alexandria
Memphis
Cyrene
Crete
Leptis Magna
Syracuse
Ismit
Istanbul
Adrianople
Brindisi
Vienna
Ravenna
Rome
Naples
Carthage
Milan
Cologne
Marseilles
Lyons
Narbonne
Timgad
Paris
London
Exeter
York
Mérida
Cartagena
Cadiz
Tangiers

Spain

After Italy, Spain was historically the most important province of the empire, though, after the conquest of Africa and the latter's establishment as the granary of Rome, it lost something of its pre-eminence. Nevertheless it remained the most urbane and civilised of the European provinces, was the home of many great Romans, among them the Emperors Trajan and Hadrian and the playwright and philosopher Seneca, and was for long the single greatest source of mineral wealth available to the Romans.

The road out of Genoa was a continuation of the Via Aurelia, but on crossing the frontier into Spain this long Mediterranean route, which had been begun about 120 B.C., took the name of Via Augusta, after the great Emperor Augustus. From Tarragona it pressed southwards until in the first year of the Christian era it reached Cartagena, the former Carthaginian colony of Carthago Nova. In the mountainous terrain through which the road often passed the work of the builders was difficult and the ground often needed various preparatory works such as retaining walls to hold back slips of loose soil or boulders, or to buttress the foundations of the wall itself during the winter rains. Often the route was crossed by streams or rivulets which were liable to become raging torrents at certain times of year, and every one had to be bridged. Yet despite obstructions roads were built crossing the peninsula in all directions.

From Tarragona a road travelled west through Saragossa and Burgos to the northern and western coasts. Down the west coast the road linked Oporto, Coimbra, Lisbon and the southern coast near the modern town of Faro. From here it ran inland to the town of Italica, home of the emperors, on the River Guadalquivir, and then south to Seville and Cadiz on the coast. The numerous overland routes included roads to Toledo and Augusta Emerita (modern Mérida), the capital of the province of Lusitania. As elsewhere in the empire the roads in Spain were used as communication routes and for military movements, but they were also a vital service to the mining industry which made the province so important in the economy of the empire. Apart from the copper mines in the region of the Rio Tinto (still mined today), there were also rich silver workings, lead mines in the Sierra Morena, south of Madrid, and mercury and cinnabar from the mines of Almaden, still one of the most important sources of the metal, in New Castile.

Africa and the roads to the east

From Cadiz the coast road ran down to Baelo at the southern tip of the peninsula and across the narrow straits, where lay the mysterious

continent of Africa which for the Romans meant effectively the north coast
of the continent as we know it today, including Egypt.

In the early centuries of her history Rome had been limited in the
Mediterranean by the maritime power of Carthage. This great city, whose
site was near the modern town of Tunis, had controlled the major ports
on the North African coast, large areas of southern Spain, the Balearic
islands, Sardinia and other territories. By about 260 B.C., however, Rome
felt strong enough to pit her strength against this rival power and there
began a series of wars that were to last until the utter obliteration of
Carthage from the map in 146 B.C. Until the end of the third century,
however, the issue was in the balance and following Hannibal's campaigns
Rome seemed on the verge of defeat. Hannibal was in charge of the army
in Spain and his heroic march through France and over the Alps into
Italy followed in the first part of its length the route later used by the Via
Augusta. After his failure before Rome and defeat in Africa, Carthage
never recovered and by the end of the second century B.C. North Africa
was a Roman province stamped with the mark of that empire—the road.
Where possible old roads were taken over and remade to Roman specifications and generally the demands of the terrain and the climate were
less stringent than those of Italy. In many stretches the engineers simply
dug down below the surface to the level of limestone or sandstone to lay
the road bed on that; in some cases, finding that the earth of the desert
hardened rapidly after rainfall, they were content to tamp down the surface
and make that into the road. In other cases, particularly where the road
approached a city, the streets and roads were paved with shaped slabs of
granite. It was not, however, until the end of the first century A.D. that
the Romans completed the road along the north coast of the continent,
linking the numerous ports that had hitherto been islands in a sea of sand.

The order to start the work was given by the Emperor Nerva in A.D. 98
and was completed fifteen years later under Trajan, who went to
Africa to supervise the final stages. The Via Nerva, as it was called, ran
from Carthage to the land of the 'three cities' or Tripolis, passing through
Sabratha, Oea and terminating in Leptis Magna. Westward from Carthage
it wended its way along the coast towards the Pillars of Hercules; eastwards
from Leptis Magna it was forced through to Alexandria. From there to
Carthage was a distance of some 1,400 miles and the building of the Via
Nerva Traiana, as the whole road was called, was one of the heroic achievements of Roman civil engineering.

The conditions of weather and terrain were often punishing and generally men of the local Berber population were impressed to do the work.
Sand dunes had to be levelled, surface soil excavated to find the bedrock,
coarse desert grass and gnarled, withered tree trunks cleared to keep the
road straight. For long stretches between the infrequent oases, wells had

to be dug at twenty-mile intervals for the travellers and their beasts, and as the road pressed out from the great city of Leptis Magna security became a major concern. Always the builder was in danger from sudden raids by the tribes of the interior, which had hoped to take over the trade of Carthage on her defeat. The prosperous coastal communities and the road that served them had to be protected by fortified frontier posts.

But more perverse than any of these hardships were the dried-up river courses or *wadis*. These, though empty for most of the year, had nevertheless to be bridged and even provided with containing walls and dams against the few weeks every year when they were flooded by the water pouring down from the mountains. The dangers that the Roman builders had to guard against were most recently realised in the autumn of 1969 when Tunisia was deluged by flood-waters. Hundreds of people were killed and at least 100,000 rendered homeless; in addition, the Tunisian economy was set back an estimated five years. In these floods a number of bridges built by Roman engineers were carried away—bridges that had still been in use up to the day of their destruction.

But there was more than just the one coastal road in Africa. In the hinterland of Carthage was an extensive network and from most of the major coastal ports little ribbons stretched back, sometimes 100 miles or more, serving the outlying frontier posts and more remote centres. Once the road reached Egypt much traffic took to the river and the broad streams of its delta. But for the Roman road-builder Egypt was only another staging post; routes ran on from across the top of the Sinai peninsula to the fabulous rock city of Petra or down the coasts of the Red Sea to serve the trade from the mysterious and distant Indies.

At the head of the north-eastern arm of the Red Sea lay the great port of Aqaba, a trading entrepôt from at least 1000 B.C. and now the port of Jordan. From here the road ran through Petra to Damascus, 400 miles to the north. It was built on the orders of the Emperor Trajan, Rome's greatest road-builder, in the early decades of the second century A.D. and ran for part of its length parallel to the River Jordan. From Aqaba the merchandise was carried by caravan northward to the great ports of the Syrian coast, such as Tyre and Antioch, whence it might be shipped to Rome. Antioch also lay at the end of another road from the east which started at the head of the Persian Gulf and ran up the Tigris before striding westward across the Syrian desert. The extent of the empire's roads is as astonishing as their excellence; everywhere within her far-ranging boundaries Rome opened the arteries of communications and commerce. Pepper, slaves and ivory from the east, ivory, slaves and wild animals from the heart of Africa for the ceaseless and bloody delights of the circus—all mixed on their way to the world's capital with imperial messengers, governors travelling to take up new commissions or returning to render their account to the senate, and, of course, with soldiers moving to defend the frontiers or to put down rebellion.

Roman roads in Britain

Research into Roman roads in Britain has been more thorough than anywhere else and, thanks to two classic books, the subject is one of the most fully documented in British archaeology. Thomas Codrington's book, published in 1903, was only superseded some fifty years later by the monumental work of Ivan D. Margary (*Roman Roads in Britain* [1955]) which attempted the huge task of documenting every stretch of Roman road still known. The resulting survey revealed a network of some 7,400 miles of road which provided over the three centuries of its building and use the most thorough communications system that Britain was to enjoy for a thousand years and more.

The roads of Roman Britain were not only well built and well surveyed, they were perfectly adapted to their function. Indeed, since the road system of the Roman province was custom-built to purposes defined by the builders, it was probably the finest system Britain has ever had. Whereas the modern road-planner has to take into account a large number of conflicting requirements and interests in his attempt to serve the needs of the community, the Roman surveyors and engineers had to consider only the needs of the imperial power, while their only rival interests were those that would grow up around the fact of the road.

We have already touched on the techniques of survey in the previous chapter but it is worth emphasising here the considerable achievement represented by these early engineers. Unaided by either compass or map and working often through heavily wooded country, they were able to lay out the shortest and most convenient routes so unfalteringly that in many cases they were followed centuries later by the railway builders. Indeed, in so far as the roads were laid out artificially to link existing or newly founded centres, rather than being the result of generations of journeys along whose course settlements had grown, they are more like a railway network than a road system. After the first stages of the conquest had been completed, the first roads to be built would be for military patrol and communications; but these were followed by routes opened up by the civil authorities for trade and to link the farms and villas with the markets of the local towns.

The same techniques would have been used in laying out these secondary roads and the survey might have been done by the same men, the local garrison commander lending surveyors from his pioneer corps to the civil authorities for the job. Such 'farm to market' roads differed from their military cousins not only in their purpose but also in their appearance and alignment. The long straight alignments of the military roads are found less frequently on these civil routes which tend to follow the natural contours of the country. It was in this part of the network that the Roman builders might also incorporate the ancient trackways used for generations by the conquered inhabitants; in such cases, although the routes were little altered the surface would be brought up to Roman standards.

In general the Roman surveyor liked to make a change of alignment on a high point which gave a good view of the surrounding countryside and assisted a distant siting for the next long stretch. It is the sharp angles of these changes of direction which give a road map of Roman Britain such a military flavour, since the road runs straight up to the turn rather than sweeping round it in a gentle curve.

After the surveyors had marked out the line of the road through the country and the ground had been cleared of brushwood, trees and other vegetation, the next stage was probably the excavation of boundary trenches that served to define the area of the road and to warn off trespassers. These small ditches, shallow and only between two and four feet wide, have been found running alongside roads still in a fair state of preservation, and it is assumed that they were a general feature of any major Roman road. Possibly intended for drainage and separated from the road by a flat open space several feet in width, they may also have served not only as boundary markers but also as a minor defensive obstacle to break the force of a chariot charge against a column marching along the road.

It could also be that there was a secondary, defensive, purpose behind the *agger* itself, the most prominent aspect of the road. This *agger* was a bank, sometimes as much as four or five feet high and fifty feet wide, that carried the road high above the countryside. Usually it was built up from the soil excavated from the drainage ditches on either side, though sometimes it was carefully constructed of stones, and its own primary function was presumably also to provide drainage for the road surface. Yet it does not seem that this was always the case, since even roads crossing high land and well-drained uplands are provided with an *agger*. The Roman empire was maintained only by continual vigilance and the frequent exercise of force; in the years immediately following a conquest the military had naturally to be prepared for risings of the local population and the roads and troops travelling along them to the source of the trouble, were all too vulnerable to attack. Little could be done against a well-prepared ambush but at least the troops could be given the advantage of the land by the slight protection of the ditches that flanked the road and by the vital extra feet in height that would enable them to fight down on their attackers.

The width of the roads varied considerably according to the traffic they had to carry, and there are indications that the Romans had a standard for the major and minor roads; Dr Margary's measurements of the width between the outer ditches satisfied him that there were probably two main types of road—one with a width of about eighty-four feet between the centres of the outer ditches, and the other with a distance of only sixty-two feet. The width of the road surface itself seems to have varied more: up to thirty feet on major routes and as little as ten or twelve feet in mountainous or otherwise difficult country. (The most common width seems to be between fifteen and eighteen feet.) The *agger* would extend a number of feet out on either side of the metalled surface although in a few instances where the road ran through well-drained peaceful country, or perhaps where it was only a very minor route, the road surface was laid directly on to the ground with little or no preparation.

Thanks to the excellence of their engineering there are still stretches of Roman roads in Britain today that have survived the rigours of a damp climate and centuries of disuse—such as the fine example at Blackstone Edge between Rochdale and Halifax. More commonly, however, the physical remains of this great system are only to be found in the straight low dykes which run for miles through the countryside like early railway embankments, and which were formerly the *aggers*. Elsewhere the researcher has to rely on differences in the vegetation above a now-sunken stretch of road and must resort to aerial photography to reveal long-obscured routes. In those instances where the Roman road was used subsequently by turnpikes in the eighteenth century and then by main trunk routes in the twentieth, nothing survives save the alignment. But even here the motorist has an uncanny sense of reaching back into the past as he drives for mile upon mile along an undeviating stretch of road; then, just as he begins to wonder whether the road will indeed go on for ever, he sees a bend ahead and, as he swings off the line, he will probably see it continuing down a green lane between the hedgerows and across the fields. If he has time and inclination to pull in and walk back he will perhaps find that this humble farm track is the very route that the legions of Rome once marched along.

Today there are maps and route guides, such as those in Dr Margary's book or the Ordnance Survey map of Roman Britain, to help the amateur in search of the roads of the ancient province. For the Roman official going about imperial business in the distant unfamiliar parts of the empire, there were very similar route maps or guides. We have mentioned the Peutinger Table in a previous chapter. This originally covered Britain as it did the rest of the empire but that portion is now lost. The best surviving document is the Antonine Itinerary which lists fifteen of the main routes, giving distances between the main halting places. Among the more

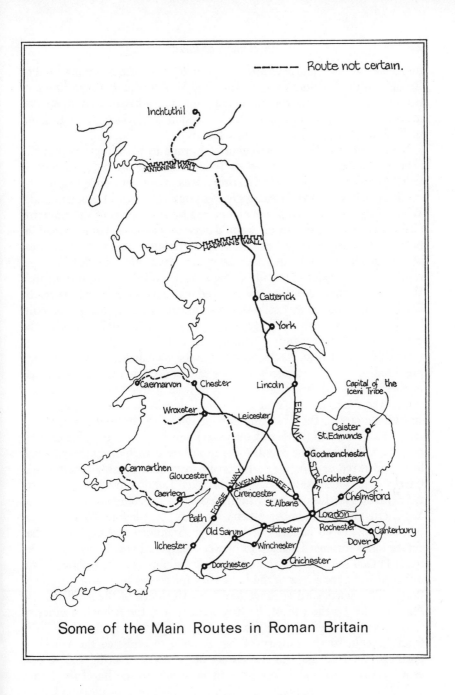

Inchtuthil

ANTONINE WALL

HADRIAN'S WALL

Catterick

York

Caernarvon   Chester   Lincoln   Capital of the Iceni Tribe

Wroxeter   Leicester   ERMINE STREET

Caister St. Edmunds

Godmanchester

Carmarthen   Gloucester   AKEMAN STREET   Colchester

Caerleon   FOSSE WAY   Cirencester   St. Albans   Chelmsford

Bath   London

Old Sarum   Silchester   Rochester   Canterbury

Ilchester   Winchester   Dover

Dorchester   Chichester

Some of the Main Routes in Roman Britain

important of these journeys are the 159 miles from the Antonine Wall to Brough on the Humber estuary; from the Wall to Richborough in Kent, one of the major ports for the voyage to Gaul, a distance of about 500 miles; from London to Dover; from London to Carlisle; from London to York; and from Caernarvon to Chester.

Britain was the last major region of Europe to be brought within the orbit of Rome. The expedition of Julius Caesar in 55 B.C., although it failed to make any conquest of territory, was important in opening up the northern island to the increasingly vigorous activities of Roman trade. When therefore the island was conquered by the armies of the Emperor Claudius in A.D. 43, the invaders could draw on a good deal of information, both from Latin merchants as well as from friendly natives. The conquest was not made overnight and the road system gradually extended from the south-east in support of the advancing armies until the whole of England, Wales and southern Scotland was covered with a network of military roads. During the centuries that followed, a secondary series of roads was built, between and across the military system, to serve the requirements of the growing trade and expanding manufactures of the province.

The first point to strike the observer is the very density of the coverage provided by the known roads, and we cannot exclude the possibility that further studies will bring other routes to light. After London the largest towns were Verulamium, near St Albans, Lincoln and York to the north; and Gloucester to the west; the port of Dover to the south and, to the east, Camulodunum (modern Colchester), one of the major tribal capitals before the Romans. The country was also covered with innumerable small forts and three or four major legionary fortresses, notably Chester and Caerleon, in South Wales. Main roads linked London to all these important centres. Northwards ran Ermine Street to Lincoln and thence up to York, crossing the Humber estuary by ferry; just before York the road branched off to go farther north through Stamford and on for another eighty miles through Durham to Newcastle upon Tyne. North again the roads fanned out to Berwick and towards Edinburgh, while above this a military road gave access to the Legionary fortress at Inchtuthill, north of Perth. This northward advance had been the work of the great general Agricola and by the end of the first century A.D. the Roman frontier in Britain had progressed from its first line, roughly along the Fosse Way from Lincoln to the estuary of the Severn, to embrace the whole of northern England and the Lowlands of Scotland. During the second century A.D. the frontier was brought back first to the line from South Shields to Carlisle, marked and defended by the great fortification known as Hadrian's Wall, and then pushed northwards again to the Antonine Wall between the Forth and the Clyde. The northern frontier was subject to periodic troubles but, thanks to the roads built to serve them, the legions were able to move freely and fast to reinforce the wall garrisons when need arose. It was not until the late fourth century, and then only when the garrisons had been weakened by ambitious generals aiming to interfere in continental politics, that the barbarian tribes began to make really serious forays into the province.

5

The Roads of Medieval Europe

DURING THE PERIOD that followed the final breakdown of Roman imperial authority in the fifth century there was neither the technology nor the will to maintain the superb highways that had been its scaffolding. In some parts of Europe their foundations remained and occasionally served as the base for later works, but in the society that sprang up in the wake of the Germanic invasions their *raison d'être* had, by and large, gone. In the north the settlements of the conquerors tended to spring up on the banks of navigable waterways, and only in the south, notably in Italy itself and Spain, did the Gothic successor states consciously attempt to maintain the cities. In much of Gaul city life was displaced as the focus of society by the great rural estates which had sprung up round the villas of the later Roman empire. But more important than the new pattern of settlement was the fact that the central authority which the Roman network had served, and by which it had been maintained, had collapsed. Roads which enabled troops, messengers or officials to travel at high speed from York to Constantinople had little value in a Europe where that route now ran through a patchwork of independent and warring statelets. Here again we find how a great road, no matter how essentially simple its engineering may be, is by its very existence a statement expressing conditions of political power without which it could not exist. In Europe, when those conditions ceased, the roads decayed.

We should also remember the crucial points of difference between the society of Europe during the Roman period and that which succeeded it. Feudal society, however varied it might be in different parts of Europe and however carefully we may need to avoid general statements as to its nature, did embody features which were fundamentally different from those of the Europe for which Rome built her roads and over which she ruled. Feudalism meant, first, numerous, virtually autonomous, local districts owing nominal allegiance to a usually ineffective central authority. It meant secondly a rural society. Both points are important. A powerful central authority is vital for an extensive road system but still more significant is the fact that Rome was an empire of cities. The most startling thing that the Romans did, and one which was so revolutionary that it did not take root for a thousand years, was to carry the idea of a city-based civilisation—the foundation of Mediterranean and Middle Eastern civilisation for two thousand years—north of the Alps.

The early Middle Ages

Everywhere Rome had gone she had built cities: their achievement in terms of urban planning and building was, and remains, quite staggering. Without precedent they imposed a pattern of towns and trading in an area which had hardly known either. And linking the cities were roads. But once the cities had fallen into disuse and Rome no longer sent legions, nor messengers with their orders, to the frontier posts, the roads had, as it were, nowhere to go. The Germanic tribes who supplanted the Romans tended to avoid the cities. Their lives were occupied with war or the hunt, and their courts tended to be itinerant. There was no single centre to administer even the small states that they set up and the concept of a well-ordered communication network had no relevance to this new society.

Nowhere was this more true than in Britain. The island was divided between a number of petty kings whose domains were separated from one another by extensive forest and marsh lands; such contacts as existed were made at first in war and only gradually through the processes of trade. The concept of the king's peace, on which was built the whole edifice of medieval law, dramatically embodied the conditions of banditry and vendetta that were commonplace. The first step of royal justice was to ensure that the king's presence should not be violated by murder and everywhere the elementary right to stay alive could be safeguarded only in the vicinity of a powerful man. Travel was hazardous in the extreme and one of the most glowing tributes by the contemporary of any early medieval king was that during his reign a woman or an unarmed merchant could journey freely without fear of their life. In a society where even the person of the traveller could not be assured it is hardly surprising that the roads on which he travelled were not maintained.

The situation again became worse during the eighth and ninth centuries. The Vikings from the north, Magyars from the east and Saracens from the south all plundered the timid civilisation that their Germanic predecessors had begun to erect on the ruins of Rome. Disruption and danger were the norm of life, free passage was a rarity and road building virtually non-existent. It was not until the somewhat more settled conditions of the later tenth century that trade and overland travel began to expand and it is at this point that we take up again the history of a road system.

The later Middle Ages

Yet as we do so we must remember that throughout the Middle Ages, and beyond, the word 'road' is more correctly understood as a right of way free from physical obstructions. Central authority struggled to maintain this right, and deputed to local communities the job of keeping the way open, of clearing fallen trees, of cutting back encroaching vegetation, of repairing and maintaining bridges. From the tenth century on, the roads of Europe were thronged with traffic of the most diverse kinds, and although even as late as the fifteenth century much trade, even from the ports on the west coast of Italy to the towns of Flanders, was still carried by sea, the overland routes were increasingly used. Yet although the traffic was comparatively heavy, little or no attempt at road maintenance was made even along those stretches that still followed the line of some long since overgrown Roman road. Furthermore, both towns and lords exacted tolls on the traffic passing over certain roads or along the rivers through their territories. Little of this money was used in road improvement; such tolls were regarded more as an outright source of revenue, the common fate of road taxes in other periods.

Nevertheless, for the road to be used at all it had to be passable or other routes would be used, and in one aspect tolls were strictly applied to the purpose for which they were levied: this was in the building of the stone bridges, many of which, such as the famous one at Totnes in Devon, are still in use today. The levy, known as 'pontage', was payable by all vehicles, save those of the king or his officers, passing over such a bridge, and the local obligation to maintain the bridges in its area was strictly enforced. Nor was bridge-building confined to such relatively easy terrain as the undulating countryside of Britain. When the 7,000-foot-high St Gotthard pass in the southern Swiss Alps was opened to traffic as early as the thirteenth century the works included the building of a bridge able to carry pack animals over the Schollenen gorge. A century later, such was the pressure of the commercial interest generated by the Italian towns, a road able to take wheeled vehicles was opened through the Septimer pass.

Yet such instances were exceptional. The governments and people of Europe were largely content with roads on which a wagoner was pleased if he could put thirty miles behind him in a day. A return to the principles of scientific road-making had to await the dilettante interest of the sixteenth century in the roads of ancient Rome, while effective application of those principles was not to begin for another century or more. Consequently our interest in this chapter will be concentrated rather on what the men of the Middle Ages were able to do about the inadequate system of land communication that they had inherited than on matters of technical advance.

Although the conditions of medieval roads were fractionally better than those of the seventeenth and eighteenth century, they were often little better than dirt tracks, dusty in summer and virtually impassable quagmires in winter. To such conditions under foot we must add the stench of decaying horse manure and, at certain times of the year when cattle were being driven to market, quantities of cow-dung. The local districts had the obligation of keeping the highways open but this meant little more than clearing the worst of the debris and cutting back encroaching undergrowth. Occasionally, when certain stretches became impossibly obstructed, repair work of the most rudimentary kind would be undertaken, either at the command of the central government or by interested parties. For any town that depended on trade for its wealth, and by definition this applied to almost all towns, the state of the approach roads was obviously a matter of concern. Occasionally, the citizens of a great trading city saw to the repair of roads miles distant. In the fourteenth century the Flemish town of Ghent made good several miles of the Ghent road leading out of Paris. So that not only the obligation by law to keep open the king's highway for the easy passage of him, his messengers or his subjects, but also self-interest combined to ensure that the necessary minimum of maintenance work was done on the more important routes.

It was in constant travel over roads such as these that the kings of Europe conducted much of their state business, for the medieval court was continually on the move. Sometimes it was in the business of war; but even in times of peace an active monarch would be restlessly travelling his dominions, investigating conditions in his realm, administering justice or merely taking rents in kind from the great magnates through whose land he passed and whose obligation it was to lodge and feed the royal retinue on demand. (The example of Henry II, king of England and lord of half France, is notorious but by no means unique.) And on these endless journeys were also to be found important administrative officials and many of the documents and records of state business. Parliaments were held at Northampton or Oxford, ceremonial 'crown wearings' at Winchester or Westminster, and many a remote part of the kingdom might find itself, for the time being, the site of the king's court. As the Middle Ages progressed, the roads of England saw a new form of travelling justice, the justices in eyre, each with his own circuit on which he conducted the business of the king's court in town after town. Nor was it only monarchs and their officers whose saddle was their office. Any great lord might own numerous manors and would expect to move from one to another, supervising his affairs in person and supporting his entourage on the produce of the locality.

Churchmen and pilgrims

The itinerary of a bishop or other religious lord would parallel that of his lay brother, but any reasonably conscientious cleric would have many other additional calls for travel. It was customary for newly appointed bishops to go to Rome if at all possible to receive their pallium, and during the course of his official life an important churchman might travel to the holy city on many other types of business. As early as the seventh century we hear of the litigious Wilfrid of York making the journey no less than three times to plead the case for the primacy of his see over that of Canterbury. From Rome came an endless stream of missionary churchmen, of papal legates going to distant parts of Europe to represent the pope in important matters, and of many lesser priests, of whose numerous missions not the least important was the collecting of church revenues. When any great dignitary, whether ecclesiastic or lay, made a journey he would be attended by a large retinue; when a royal lady was moving her court to that of a new husband she would be attended by many servants, by courtiers and possibly poets and musicians; when a king sent an embassy it would be numerous and impressive. When the business of the great called them to travel, the merchants, wandering scholars and friars, the travelling journeymen and masons, and the throngs of pilgrims on the road were sure of a spectacular sight—if also of difficulty in getting accommodation.

Pilgrimage was probably the largest single factor, affecting all classes of society, to generate traffic along the roads of Europe from the twelfth century onwards. The idea of earning absolution of sin or spiritual capital in the next world by travelling to the sites of martyrdom and saintly relics in this one, had gained increasing popularity from the mood of spiritual revival generated by the founding of the great monastery of Cluny in the first years of the tenth century. Soon penitents of all social ranks were journeying to the various shrines of Europe and by the beginning of the eleventh century many were taking the arduous road to Jerusalem itself. When the control of the holy places passed from the hands of the tolerant and amenable Abbasid dynasty of Arab rulers to a more fanatical race, the fate of the cradle of Christendom became a matter of concern to thousands of ordinary people, now denied this supreme act of grace. It should be understood that although the goal of the journey was to witness the relics and holy places themselves the very fact of travelling so many hundreds of miles over the difficult and dangerous roads was an action of merit. In the tenth century the notorious Fulk Nerra, Count of Anjou, had hoped to earn forgiveness for a life of continual brigandage by making the pilgrimage to Jerusalem but had died on the journey. By the time Pope Urban II preached the First Crusade in 1087 his message appealed not only to the martial and acquisitive instincts of the lesser nobility, the descendants of Fulk and his kind, but also reached the hearts of many ordinary and pious folk.

The tradition of popular pilgrimage established in the tenth century and then so rudely broken must be seen as an important factor in the tremendous response to the pope's message, preached throughout Europe by wandering priests and special emissaries. In 1099 Jerusalem, the city of Christ's passion, and Bethlehem, the village of his birth, had been recovered by the warriors of the Cross and from then on for three generations the roads to the Holy Land were busy with traffic of pilgrimage. In Europe itself guest-houses and monasteries along the route catered for the needs of the pilgrims, while on the dangerous roads of Asia Minor and Syria, open to attack by local brigands and Islamic soldiers, the two military orders of the Hospital and the Temple were founded and dedicated to the protection and succour of the travellers.

Rome and Jerusalem were by no means the only centres of pilgrimage and in the eleventh century another shrine came to rival them in popularity. This was the church of Santiago de Compostela in the north-west corner of Spain; it housed, so it was claimed, the body of St James himself, one of Christ's apostles. Routes led from all parts of northern and eastern France to converge on the pass of Roncesvalles in the Pyrenees; thence the road lay via Burgos, Leon and Villafranca to Santiago. The main routes were from Paris and Vézelay on the Seine, and Lyons and Arles on the Rhône; at these termini pilgrims from all over eastern and northern Europe would gather to prepare for the long journey ahead of them. The roads were no doubt as badly surfaced as any others during the period but the pilgrims were well served with information and could expect good accommodation on the road. For along each route there were many other important shrines. The religious tourist from Germany, say, could 'take in' the abbey of St Denis at Paris and the church of St Martin at Tours on his way south to Spain and return by another route to the borders of the empire, visiting the abbey of St Martial at Limoges, famed for its music, and the great church at Vézelay. These and many other shrines invited his attention and alms, and were fully described in the many itineraries or guide-books written for pilgrims. Churches were built to accommodate the relics; aisles gave easy passage to the crowds of pilgrims who daily walked slowly past to see the relics. At each halting place there would be a large number of hostelries catering to all tastes. In addition to the fairly high standard of accommodation that they could expect, the pilgrims were comparatively free from the attentions of bandits —not because of their holy occupation but because they usually travelled in large companies and would often number among them knights or professional men-at-arms.

Vehicles and travellers

Although the poor state of the roads of medieval Europe can hardly be doubted, it is perhaps significant that, compared with the torrent of abuse showered on the roads by the travellers of the seventeenth and eighteenth centuries, the men of the Middle Ages seem to have been far less given to criticism. Of course we have only the surviving sources to go on and these do contain evidence that the authorities sometimes felt the need to improve conditions. Nevertheless it is possible that the roads of Europe between the tenth and sixteenth centuries were more suited to the demands made on them than was later to be the case. There is some scientific evidence that the general climatic conditions took a turn for the worse in the fifteenth century. We know, for instance, that the vine was cultivated in England until this period and there are other hints that rainfall in northern Europe was generally less than in later centuries.

Somewhat less speculative is the fact that wheeled traffic was far less common and wheeled passenger traffic virtually unknown. Not until the reign of Elizabeth I did the English monarch have an official travelling coach and before that time in England, as in much of Europe, even the greatest men in the realm expected to do their travelling on horseback. The fourteenth-century Luttrell Psalter has an illustration of a heavy travelling carriage used by the ladies of the Luttrell family, while in the middle years of the same century a great lady bequeathed to her eldest daughter 'her great carriage with the couvertures and cushions'. And if the monarch did not use a coach, his queen often did. Two years before his deposition Richard II's exchequer paid out no less than £400 for the making of the queen's 'chariot'; a sum that would have purchased a herd of eight hundred fine cows.

Yet for the most part the upper classes travelled by horseback, both men and women, fit and sickly. In the 1440s Margaret Paston wrote to her husband, taken ill in London, to return to Norfolk as soon as he was well enough to ride; Chaucer's Prioress, like all the other pilgrims on that boisterous pilgrimage, rode a horse. It is possible that the gentle Madame Eglantyne, whose innocent pretensions Chaucer recounts so lovingly, may have followed the new fashion among ladies of riding side-saddle. Yet the fashion was by no means general in the later fourteenth century and, if her French is anything to go by, it is probable that the Prioress would not even have known about it. By and large, then, the gentry took to the saddle if they intended to travel, while lesser folk walked.

For the transport of goods the pack-horse was the general rule; though carts were not uncommon for the heavier and bulkier commodities such as wheat. Indeed, they were an essential part of the equipment of a large farm and could be hired at comparatively reasonable rates; wheat would be carried at a charge of about one penny per ton mile. As often as not the owner would find his valuable if clumsy vehicle, its wheels shod with iron nails to make them sturdier and grip the road better, commandeered by the royal purveyors or the agents of the powerful local lord. The constant movement of the royal courts demanded transport and if the king himself and his immediate entourage could look to a comparatively rapid and easy journey on well-fed and well-groomed horses, their effects had to be transported in the lumbering vehicles taken from the farmyard. And it was not only authorised royal or noble agents that the landowners had to fear. There were plenty of impostors ready, with a show of strength, to claim royal authority to requisition goods and transport. The authorities tried to stop this unauthorised drain on their subjects' resources and during the fourteenth century one after another of the French kings issued edicts forbidding anyone to attempt to act in this way without up-dated royal letters patent.

Horse-power

Naturally, all the transport we have described depended, as it had for centuries, on horse-power. Like the internal combustion engine, the horse needed regular and skilled attention to produce its best performance. The modern frequency of the surname Smith is an indication of how important the local smithy was. His responsibility extended not only to the needs of travellers and their mounts, for whom he provided the equivalent of the modern garage breakdown service, but also to the repair and maintenance of farm equipment and farm horses. The smithy was a central feature of medieval travel.

Any great household had a complete staff of officers primarily respons- ible for travel and transport, as we see from Margaret Labarge's fascinat- ing book *A Baronial Household of the Thirteenth Century*. The marshal was responsible for the supply of fodder and shoeing iron for the horses, one of his clerks saw to the maintenance of any heavy carts on the manor and kept an eye on the working capacity of the horses, while yet another paid the grooms. The household smith was kept fully occupied and fully supervised, since an important point of employing a household smith was to avoid the sharp practice of the public smithy. In France, for example, the tale was told of smiths who, when shoeing a traveller's horse, drove a small spike into its hoof. A couple of miles down the road, the horse became completely lame and the rider would find himself being offered a derisory price for the beast by a 'knacker' who would happen to be passing and was, of course, working with the smith. The horse after being rested for a couple of days could then be sold at its market value.

During the Middle Ages there were a far wider variety of horses in general use than is common today and breeding was of necessity a well-understood art. The famous war-horses, or destriers, could carry a fully-armed knight, weighing between two and three hundredweight, into a charge. But there also were the high-stepping palfreys of the ladies; hunters; cart-horses; and sumpter horses, which might be expected to carry all the effects of a sizeable household on the move. It was pack-horses of this type that were used by merchants. From the north of Europe caravans of them made their arduous way through the difficult routes of central Europe and up the winding and inhospitable tracks of the Alps down into the Po valley of Italy, coming to a halt at one of the great Italian towns. Here they would meet other merchants who weeks before had disembarked at one of the Italian Adriatic ports to set out on the last lap of their journey to one of the great northern entrepôts like Pavia. Then began the tricky and expert business of barter. On the long journey to his ultimate destination the merchant had to contend with the danger of plunder from bandits or impoverished petty noblemen; he would have had to pay many heavy tolls, tolls which were frequently simply protection money, and of course he had to contend with the roads themselves. Then at the end of the journey, once safely completed, was this last great hazard.

A man might make his fortune as a trader, he might end up in a debtors prison, he might spend his life enjoying average but never brilliant success—all depended now on his knowledge of the market and the skill with which he could profit from the horses, slaves, woollens and linens that he had brought from the north.

Maintenance and hazards

Attempts were made by the authorities from time to time to improve the condition of the roads. In 1353 Edward III issued instructions that the road between Temple Bar and Westminster was to be resurfaced, since although it was supposedly already a paved road it had become virtually impassable to traffic. The landowners on either side were to be responsible for making good a footpath seven feet wide, while the central strip was to

1

The motor roads built by Mussolini's engineers in the 1920s often followed the routes of ancient Roman roads. Notice the way in which the paving stones were shaped so that they formed a a continuous surface.

2

The Via Appia was lined with tombs like the one shown here. They were a subject of rival display among the rich families of the capital, and their sumptuous decoration made them a popular tourist attraction in the ancient world.

3 The livery of the Royal Mail coaches, showing the emblems of the orders of chivalry and the royal coat of arms, together with their superbly groomed horses, made them a brilliant sight. The running times of the coaches were improved by limiting the number of outside passengers or forbidding them altogether.

4
Highwaymen, like James Whitney shown here, were treated as heroes by all classes of eighteenth-century society.

5 The condition of the roads in the eighteenth century led wagon-builders to design vehicles with huge 'dished' wheels. With its cambered rim the wheel, which was wide enough to ride most of the ruts in the road, was also in contact with the road across its entire surface.

THE PAVIER

6 The careful grading of the stones to a standard size, required by the techniques of road-building introduced at the end of the eighteenth century, demanded an army of labourers as stone-breakers. The pavier, who rammed home the surface, was something of a skilled artisan.

7 The old toll-gate at Notting Hill, from which the modern district of London received its name.

8 During the nineteenth century more and more turnpikes were abolished; for the citizens of Devizes in 1868 this was obviously an occasion for celebrations on the grand scale.

9 England was not the only country plagued with highwaymen during the eighteenth century, as this scene on an Italian road shows.

10 The drama of the Alpine roads is captured by this early nineteenth-century print of the approach to the Mont Cenis pass.

11 An artist's impression of the descent of the mail coach
over the St Gotthard pass.

12 This magnificent natural bridge, in what is now the Yellowstone National Park, is called the 'rainbow turned to stone' by the Navajo Indians who used it in one of their ancient trails.

13 An American wagon train. Emigrants crossing the Plains in the shadow of the Rocky mountains. (A Currier & Ives lithograph, after F. F. Palmer.)

14 The turnpike at Harrodsburg, Kentucky, in 1885.

15 Road conditions somewhat less than ideal two miles beyond the city limits of Cleveland, Ohio, on the road to Warrenville, in 1891.

be properly paved. The width is not given but it was probably sufficient for two carts to pass. In the middle of the previous century we hear of a dispute over the road at Winchcombe, threatened by an extension to the parish church; the royal court ruled that whatever extensions were made the road should be at least eighteen feet wide, since the townspeople had complained that the rector's plans for his church would prevent the carts passing one another and thus cause congestion on market day.

The condition of the road was of vital importance to the townsmen of Winchcombe as of all other market towns. This was equally true of the guilds of the capital. The City of London levied tolls from all trade entering the city to maintain the roads in the immediate environs of the capital; later in the fourteenth century we find the Provost of Paris making similar provisions and also demanding the impressment of the local citizenry to repair roads that seem to have been in a worse condition than the surrounding countryside. Indeed, it must often enough have been difficult to tell which was the road and which the fields, for the ordinance itself refers to 'ravines of water' and even to trees that had been allowed to grow up in the road.

Such ordinances were issued, from time to time, in many parts of Europe but no government made any deliberate attempt to build up an efficiently engineered road system. Rather, they had to devote most of their efforts to holding down the continuing outbreaks of lawlessness. The dangers were not merely from common robbers, later to be dignified with the term highwaymen, who lurked in the encroaching hedgerows and the woods, but also from members of the nobility. In Germany the problem was chronic throughout the thirteenth, fourteenth and fifteenth centuries and the central government, when it existed, was largely powerless. 'Land' peaces were proclaimed but to little effect and the remedy lay ultimately in the hands of the merchants and the towns. The mighty Hanseatic League was powerful enough to protect its members and in the South merchants tried to beat the landless knights at their own game by engaging one of them to fight on their behalf. To this endemic lawlessness was added the danger of footloose companies of freebooting soldiers looking for employment in one of the many wars available, or the chance of plundering unarmed merchants.

Conditions were not much better in England, where the central authority was among the most powerful in Europe and where counter-marching of armies was much less common and the menace of mercenaries virtually unknown. In the year 1342 a body of Lichfield merchants attempted to obtain justice against a certain Sir Robert de Rideware, Knight, who with a gang of gentlemanly companions had held them up on the road to Stafford Fair and robbed them of forty pounds' worth of 'spicery and mercery'. He had made good his crime despite the prompt action of the town bailiff who had led a posse against the knights, disbanded their followers and executed four of their number. Rideware, who does not seem to have been in any way put out by the fate of his companions, rallied more support and calmly waylaid the merchants again, retook their property and set some of his bullies to keep an eye on them.

While such episodes were possible—and they were common enough throughout Europe—we may hardly wonder that the state of the roads themselves was not in the forefront of the minds of the administration or the merchant community.

6

Roads in Britain before the Railway Age

THANKS TO A fine network of navigable waterways and the advantage of a long coastline penetrated by many inlets, Britain enjoyed perhaps the best system of natural communications of any European country. This fact alone must have contributed essentially to the sudden burst of industrial activity which, gathering strength throughout the eighteenth century, mushroomed into the Industrial Revolution. It may also help to explain how it was that until then roads in Britain had not received serious consideration from government. Ironically enough, at the very moment when the name of McAdam was becoming a household word for the excellence of a new technique of road-building, the country was poised for a fresh and breathtaking development which was to divert most of the capital investment in transport to an entirely new invention. During the age of the railways the roads of Britain were not entirely neglected, but far less was done than was needed, while the system of highway administration remained virtually as it had been during the Middle Ages.

Canals, the first modern communication network

Before turning our attention to the roads of Britain in the age of the Industrial Revolution, we should first take a look at the earlier developments in communications which did so much to accelerate and intensify that Revolution. Partly perhaps because of her excellent natural waterways Britain had lagged behind France in the pioneering of canals. For a century after its completion in 1681 there was nothing to equal the stupendous Languedoc canal between the Bay of Biscay and the Mediterranean. But, between the opening of the Sankey Brook navigation in 1760 and the 1840s, when the rail network was rapidly covering the country, it has been estimated that some 4,000 miles of canals were built in Britain.

In some ways this achievement, in terms of engineering and construction, surpassed even the heroic work of the railway builders, who were able to use increasingly effective steam-driven machinery to lighten some of their labour. For both railways and canals, most of the earth-moving and excavation was done by manual labour and by the same body of men —the 'navvies' who built the railways being the descendants of the race of giants who had been recruited for navigations or canals. The canal-builders, however, very often had more difficult and more elaborate works to contend with. There were numerous tunnels and locks, essential for carrying a level watercourse through the hilly countryside of England, and magnificent aqueducts that carried the barge traffic over rivers and high above wooded valleys. The Pont-y-Cyssyllte aqueduct, which Telford built for the Ellesmere canal at a cost of £47,000, has nineteen openings, each with a span of forty-five feet; it carried the canal a distance of some 900 feet over the River Dee, at a height of 126 feet. With such works modern Europe once again began to emulate the achievements of the Romans.

But the engineering problems in the construction of a canal did not stop at the surveying and building of a level waterway, interrupted as rarely as possible by locks. These were difficult enough, but often a canal demanded the most elaborate ancillary works; for an artificial waterway needs an assured flow of water throughout the year and cannot always depend on a sufficient rainfall. Telford and his colleagues might have to design and build vast reservoirs sited to serve the summit point of the canal and provided with a network of feeder canals.

Given such massive requirements, we may well wonder why the entrepreneurs of the eighteenth century committed themselves to the canal rather than to road improvements. Yet the canals had many advantages. First, the canal was a private 'road', and traffic could be easily limited only to authorised users. The canal era opened with the building of twenty-four miles of waterway for Francis Egerton, third Duke of Bridgewater, the 'father of British inland navigation', in the 1760s. The engineer was the famous James Brindley, who went on to design a further 350 miles of canals. Brindley himself, of a Derbyshire labouring family, had no doubt as to the value of his life's work. Once when asked by a committee what was the use of navigable rivers, he replied unhesitatingly, 'To feed canals.' The chief advantage of the canal over the river was that its direction could be determined; over the road, that it could be built for a specific function and its use limited to that function. Bridgewater commissioned his canal to bring coal from the mines on his estates to Manchester; the operation could be accurately costed and the duke, investing in a private enterprise, was not liable to see his investment deteriorate through the extensive public use to be expected on a road. Furthermore, although barges, like wagons, were horse-drawn, they were at an advantage in the matter of speed, since the plane surface of water and the absence of moving parts reduced the element of friction dramatically. Finally, the capacity of a barge was much greater than that of a wagon.

Britain's roads, on which the bulk of traffic was still pack-horses, and which were used by vast herds of cattle being taken to market on the hoof, as well as by heavy and ill-designed wagons and carriages, demanded overall planning and an effective system of maintenance and administration. The private industrialist could not wait for such decisions nor rely on them to meet his precise demands. However, at the end of the eighteenth century many hundreds of miles of good roads were built and we must now turn to the history of road-building, still very much a junior partner in the communications network of early industrial Britain.

Administration and legislation

The background to the English system of parochial responsibility for roads has been touched on in the chapter on medieval roads. It was still valid for the time when McAdam attempted to persuade the authorities of the need of some degree of centralisation—indeed, it has coloured road-planning and administration in the Britain of the 1960s. Even today the traveller will find the sign for a county boundary unmistakably underlined by a sudden change in the road surface, and the second-class roads in some parts of the country better than first-class ones in others.

The parishes, obliged to keep open the king's highway, made use of that standard method of English administration of earlier centuries, the unpaid official. A surveyor of highways was appointed each year to recruit and direct the necessary local labour and to ensure that the roads were opened up after the depredations of winter. For it was generally accepted, even when Thomas Telford was a young man, that long tracts of 'road' would be unusable by wheeled vehicles for four or five months in the year. The system of unpaid supervisors and forced labour had perhaps worked adequately during the Middle Ages when the peasant population was in any case used to working on the lord's land during certain times of the year. But as attitudes in society changed, and the principle of paid labour became general, so the dependence of road maintenance on forced labour became anachronistic, and the job of the highway surveyor increasingly difficult and even more odious. He lacked the prestige, enjoyed by the equally unpaid justice of the peace, of working directly for the king's interest, and could claim no kind of patronage or real authority.

Significantly enough, the first piece of legislation in the English statute book relating to the maintenance of the highways comes in the reign of the Tudor queen, Mary, in 1555. Significantly also, as with so many instances in the history of English road administration, it was passed as a temporary measure. Nevertheless, it attempted to define the duties of the highway surveyors and, as it gave the justice of the peace an obligation to reinforce the surveyor's authority by imposing defined penalties, it did mark an extension of the central authority. This tentative and inadequate measure remained the basic legislation on highways well into the eighteenth century (it was not in fact repealed until the 1830s).

The basic legislation was supplemented by numerous Acts to give more precision and greater force. It has been estimated that no fewer than two thousand Road Acts were passed between 1700 and 1790; the majority were Bills to set up new turnpike trusts, but many were modifications and glosses on existing Acts. A contemporary lawyer frankly admitted that there were areas of road legislation so complex that neither he nor any of his colleagues would be prepared to make a confident pronouncement on their exact significance. In any case, none of this legislation altered the fact that the system rested on the parish, and even attempts to finance important roads by a levy on the country were extremely rare. Thus the traveller journeying any distance was at the mercy of the efficiency of hundreds of small authorities who made little or no attempt at co-ordination and who all depended on forcing or cajoling unwilling parishioners into supplying their labour or their equipment gratis. Cromwell's proposal to appoint a national surveyor of the highways with sufficient funds to give meaning to his office, an unheard-of measure of rational public action, was hotly opposed.

At the time when the Industrial Revolution was beginning to change everything in English society and would soon force the country to devise a realistic system of transport, the maintenance of the public highways was the responsibility of a host of incompetent, unpaid and effectively powerless men whose activities were regulated by an almost equally numerous and equally inept body of conflicting statutes. The power of the parish and the local justice to demand reports from their surveyors and to enforce statutory labour was largely ignored. Some parishes made fitful attempts to provide their surveyors with a salary but the men chosen for the job, one universally hated, were almost without exception inadequate. There was no tradition of road-building; there was no encouragement or incentive to master a demanding profession; there was the administrative responsibility of handling such money as was available;

and, by a series of exemptions, the best-educated and wealthier residents of the parish were in any case not eligible for appointment. Finally, even in the rare cases where a surveyor took his work seriously, his term of office was gratefully relinquished at the end of a year and his place taken by another completely unprepared for the responsibilities he faced. It is not surprising that, as the eighteenth century advanced, more and more complaints against the system were heard, and new means were sought to improve it.

The turnpikes

This new system, for the upkeep of the more important public highways, was based on a number of 'turnpike' trusts which, being empowered to collect tolls for the purpose, took over the upkeep of defined stretches of road. The term turnpike derived from the form of the barrier which marked the entry to the section of the road controlled by the trust. This was originally in the form of a pivoted bar looking like a spear or pike and similar to the barriers on modern unmanned railway crossings. The trusts were established by act of parliament for a period of twenty-one years, after which time it was assumed that the road would be in a sound state of repair and could thereafter be maintained by the traditional method of parish forced labour. Yet again we find the establishment of temporary remedies and once again they proved self-perpetuating. As a matter of course the trusts applied for second and third terms and, since each new term required a new parliamentary act, involved the trust in heavy legal and parliamentary expenses. But these, as we shall see, accounted only in part for the fact that the trusts were generally heavily in debt and only a small part of the money supposedly collected for road repairs and improvement in fact went to this purpose.

The first gate was set up, by act of parliament, in 1663, in Cambridgeshire, on the London–York road. It was the result of representation to parliament by the parish authorities, who found that the costs of maintaining this busy highway were, despite their best efforts, beyond their resources. From then on more and more parishes found local worthies, anxious in the first instance to improve the roads, joining to form trusts with parliamentary licence to levy tolls. By the end of the eighteenth century more than 20,000 miles of British roads were under the supervision of turnpikes.

Before looking at the numerous drawbacks that have earned the turnpikes their bad reputation, it should first be said that for all their shortcomings they did effect real improvements in numerous sections of the road network and that contemporary travellers by and large welcomed the toll-gate as an earnest of at least a few miles of tolerable travelling conditions. As the trusts became established, so they became a part of the landscape. The original simple turnpikes were replaced by sturdy gates, and the wood-and-wattle huts of the 'pike keepers' gave place to stone-built cottages (*see* Plate 7). Many of these, often octagonal in plan and always attractive and well proportioned, are still to be seen on the roads of Britain today.

Generally popular with travellers as they were, and at first not unpopular with the communities of the local parishes, the turnpike trusts became a target for considerable and occasionally violent antipathy. For the parish did not receive any benefit from the tolls collected and soon the trusts were empowered to draw on the statute·labour—at first for payment of wages fixed by Parliament and later for a proportion of the statutory requirement, without payment. In some cases the trusts were even able to appropriate materials from the common land without payment. Finally the parish could still be held ultimately responsible for the road, and although it could in theory recover any money it had to disburse to make good work neglected by the trust, in fact the latter was so largely in debt that the parish had little hope of repayment. The position was the worse since the members of the trust were generally the most influential members of the local community and, as like as not, on the parish council themselves.

The situation eventually became so tense that destruction of a toll-house was added to the lengthening list of offences punishable by death. But despite their privileges and apparent power the trusts were rarely profit-making bodies. In almost every case they had to raise a sizeable loan even to defray the costs of getting their act of parliament, and loans were regularly floated in anticipation of revenues for any kind of expenditure so that as time went by more and more future income was mortgaged to servicing these debts. The situation was made worse by the amateurishness and frequent incompetence of the trustees in administering their affairs, and a certain amount of peculation, though it seems to have been slight, cannot be ruled out.

Worst of all, however, was the fact that the revenues were 'taxed' at source by dishonest collectors. These were not badly paid, but, lacking any machinery on the gate which could register the number of vehicles passing through, the trust had virtually no means of checking what their revenues should be. By sending out inspectors, the trustees could establish some idea of a reasonable day's takings but they had to resign themselves to the loss of any excess of that figure should the traffic increase in volume. Furthermore, since, in accordance with the universally accepted principle that the traffic should be adapted to the roads, there were numerous and heavy surcharges on vehicles overweight or with tyres below regulation width, there was plenty of scope for 'arrangements' between toll collectors and wagoners. The opportunity was not missed. As a result of their employees' dishonesty and their own inability to find any foolproof way of combating it, the trusts soon fell back on the last resort of farming the tolls. By this means they were at least spared the trouble of collecting, but since the whole point for the 'farmer' was to maximise his profits, the trust inevitably had to let the concession at a fraction of its real value.

For these reasons, then, the turnpikes were continually in debt and only a small part of the money collected for the upkeep of the road was in fact used for that purpose. Nevertheless, as we have seen, the turnpike roads were often notably better than those maintained by the parish. What was needed, of course, was some mechanism of national road policy. This seemed about to emerge at the beginning of the nineteenth century when Thomas Telford was appointed by the government to survey the London to Holyhead road. The route passed through the toll-gates of twenty-three separate turnpike trusts but the road was built, and, encouraged by this success, the government asked the great engineer to draw up plans for a similar massive improvement to the great north road from London to Edinburgh. But this and all further active central control of the country's roads was cut short by the invention of the steam locomotive and the intensive development of the railways that followed.

Thomas Telford

Thomas Telford, the son of a shepherd, was born in Eskdale, Dumfriesshire, in 1757. In his long life (he died at the age of seventy-seven) he came to epitomise the generation of engineers who were the pioneers of the astonishing new society that was being born in industrial Britain. He had no advantages in his education, yet, as a young man, following the predelictions of his society, he published a certain amount of poetry under the pseudonym of Eskdale Tam. At the age of twenty-five he went to London and there won a contract to repair the castle of Sir William Pulteney, a member of parliament for Shrewsbury. Thanks to Pulteney, he was made surveyor of public works for Salop and after his appointment as engineer for the Ellesmere canal in 1793 his career was assured. Thereafter he directed a number of major projects, including the Caledonian canal, in Britain, and was decorated with the Swedish order of knighthood of Gustavus Vasa for his design and construction of the Gotha canal between Lake Wener and the Baltic Sea. Besides canals, his contracts included harbours, bridges and drainage schemes, and it was not until the early years of the nineteenth century, when he was already forty-six, that he received his first major road contract (though he was soon to win the punning nickname of the 'colossus of Roads').

Telford made his name as a road-builder in the Highlands of Scotland. His predecessor here had been General Wade, who had laid down a system of well-engineered roads after the suppression of the Jacobite Rebellion of 1745. But, despite their technical excellence, these had been exclusively military, and served the needs of an English army rather than the Scottish communities. Telford was engaged on a socially more valuable project. The occasion was a survey commissioned by the British government, during a truce in the Napoleonic Wars. This survey was at the instance of a society founded in the latter half of the eighteenth century and dedicated to revitalising the economic and social conditions of the Highlands, following the depopulation caused by the ruthless evictions put through by the local lairds in the 1780s.

Telford's brief was not limited to a consideration of roads. His recommendations included plans for bridges and harbours and, more important, a proposal for a canal through the Great Glen which was later to mature as the Caledonian canal. As a result of Telford's comprehensive yet brilliantly detailed plans, Parliament set up commissions for the building both of the canals and also of the roads, with Telford the engineer in charge of both projects. Before 1820 he had supervised the construction of over 1,000 miles of road and many hundreds of bridges, among them such masterpieces as the bridge over the Tay.

As his brilliant and successful career advanced Telford won immense prestige both in England and abroad. In addition to the Swedish canal project, he built the Polish road from Warsaw to Brest-Litovsk for the Austrian government. He remained a bachelor throughout his life and his reputation among engineers was such that the Salopian Coffee House at Charing Cross, where he lived for some twenty years in the latter part of his career, became a recognised centre for young engineers. Indeed, it was from his base there that Telford helped found the society that became the Institute of Civil Engineers (of which he was the first president). Such was Telford's fame that he was a valuable asset to the owner of the Salopian and when he announced his intention of moving to new lodgings the proprietor, who had only recently bought the business, exclaimed: 'What, leave the house! Why, sir, I have just paid £750 for you.'

The importance of Telford's work as a road engineer was the fact that he brought sound principles of engineering to bear on the problems of road construction. In place of the haphazard and largely slipshod methods in use he insisted on careful drainage, both beneath the road surface itself and in the adjoining terrain, to prevent possible landslips that would disturb the foundations and surface. He also required the most careful grading of stones for the foundation and the surface, using uniformly sized large stones for the former, and irregular but small stones for the latter. Whereas earlier builders had attempted to bind the foundation and surface with clay or chalk (with dreadful results), Telford only used stones that were carefully washed and sieved. The surface of the pavement was moderately cambered to throw off the water without canting up the vehicles at an exaggerated angle. (Overturns were common occurrences; Arthur Young recorded passing three up-ended wagons on the short journey between Manchester and Stockport in the 1760s.) As the iron shoes of the horses and the iron tyres of the wagons ground down the sharp corners of the small stones in the upper layer, and the dust worked into the structure of the road, it was hardened and bound into a smooth and virtually watertight covering.

Besides the important network which he built in the Highlands, opening up many places that formerly had been virtually inaccessible, Telford also made an essential contribution south of the border with his magnificent highway from London to North Wales; the Menai suspension bridge, that carried it over the Straits to Anglesey, was one of his most superb achievements. The road from London to Holyhead, following roughly the route of the present A5, was in many of its sections entirely resurveyed by Telford, who also had to bear the burden of seeing all the necessary local private members' bills through Parliament and of negotiating with the local authorities and turnpike trusts along the route. Telford brought to North Wales the first decent road it had known for centuries; in the latter part of the eighteenth century a traveller described Welsh roads as rocky lanes full of stones as big as one's horse. The road took some twenty years to complete and cost £750,000, but this included the cost of the Menai bridge.

John McAdam

John Loudon McAdam was born in Ayrshire in 1756, the son of a country gentleman. His father died when he was eighteen and he went to America as an articled clerk in his uncle's office in New York. During the War of Independence he made a sizeable fortune as an agent for the sale of prizes captured from the American rebels. When, however, the rebels became the legal government of the new United States McAdam, not unnaturally, found himself penniless and returned to Europe, finally settling in Scotland in 1783. He was appointed a commissioner for highways and, unlike most men given this thankless task, made it his business to understand everything he could both about the techniques of road construction and about the system, if such it could be called, of highway administration. In the early 1800s he moved south and made his home in Bristol. His expertise was gradually becoming recognised and in 1816 he became the highway inspector for Bristol and its environs. His reputation rapidly became nation-wide, and turnpike trusts throughout Britain consulted him so that even before his death his name had become a household word for the type of road surface that he used. The importance of McAdam's contribution was also recognised by authority, and he was frequently consulted by parliamentary committees on roads as well as publishing much on his own account.

Like Telford, McAdam paid meticulous attention to the correct grading and selection of materials and to good drainage. His major contribution, a water-bound dust surface, was essentially a derivation of Telford's technique, but he dispensed almost entirely with the elaborate foundations laid by Telford. True, much of McAdam's work was in the repair of existing roads; in the few new roads that he built, however, he applied his basic principle that well-drained subsoil was fully capable of bearing any load likely to be carried on the road. The results justified his confidence, and the main objection to McAdam's system only became fully apparent with the advent of the rubber tyre and the faster speeds of motor vehicles. The heavy, slow-moving horse-drawn wagons had pulverised the stone surface effectively to provide the dust, which might be reinforced with lime, and produce a binding medium already described; they also compacted the stones even more tightly. But improved tyres and greater speeds produced very different results. The fast-moving rubber tyre tended to loosen rather than compact the stone surface while, as traffic speeds went up, the dust problem, always present to some degree on a water-bound McAdam road, became enormous. For this reason bituminous tar came to be used as the binding medium in the twentieth century, although the McAdam principle remained basically unchanged.

The main advantage of McAdam's roads over Telford's was in the cost. The great engineer designed roads to last, and over the decades of service that they gave their real cost was low, but the initial outlay was considerable and Telford had to meet contemporary criticisms on this point. By doing without the foundation, McAdam produced a surface that was both comparatively cheap and, thanks to careful drainage, had almost as long a life.

The real contribution of these men, however, and the basis of their success, was that for the first time they brought both sound engineering principles and common sense to the building of Britain's roads. The use of the camber to throw off surface water had been grasped by their predecessors, but the idea was carried to absurdity—the road was sometimes so steeply pitched that wagons frequently overturned. Furthermore, the traffic naturally tended to hug the centre of the road, which not only led to fisticuffs between drivers over who had the right of way but also meant that the crown of the road received excessive wear. McAdam advocated a camber with a rise of only three inches over a road width of eighteen feet.

Of still greater importance was the fact that both these two pioneers, and particularly Telford, consciously designed their roads for wheeled traffic. His London-to-Holyhead road had a ruling gradient of one in thirty. During the nineteenth century theorists came to accept that this gradient of one in thirty was the maximum that a horse could manage efficiently both in ascent and descent. At the same time they emphasised that a perfectly plane road was bad from the point of view of drainage and advocated a minimum gradient of one in 105 to one in 150. This kind of thinking and theorising would have been unimaginable in England at the beginning of the eighteenth century and it was largely thanks to the work of Telford and McAdam that it was standard practice at the end of the nineteenth.

The seventy years from the beginning of work on the Bridgewater canal in 1760 and the opening of the Liverpool and Manchester railway in 1830 witnessed the realignment of English society from an agricultural to an industrial base. Social attitudes changed more slowly, but the generations of Englishmen who lived under those indifferent monarchs George III and his son George IV changed the direction of their country's history, and that of the world, unalterably. During these decades England became the first society in history to reach a position of industrial take-off. Good internal communications were an essential factor in this development and we have noted the part played by the rivers and canals in the first stage of the Industrial Revolution; the railways made a vital contribution to the second. Sandwiched between these two great advances in transport the roads enjoyed only a brief period of importance.

The mail-coach service

Yet in the opening years of the nineteenth century it might have seemed that a new age of road travel had opened. Quite apart from the work of Telford and then McAdam, the inauguration of the mail-coach service by the Post Office in 1784 geared the whole system of passenger transport to a new idea of speed on the road and, above all, of punctuality. Until this year the royal mails had been carried by post-'boys' on horseback; the service was slow—the journey from Bath to London took the best part of two days—and dangerous. The riders were often held up and robbed by highwaymen and they might well be killed. Yet it was the view of the authorities that nothing could reasonably be done to improve the posts. However, they were obliged to think again when, in 1782, a stage-coach service opened between Bath and London which covered the distance in seventeen hours. Not surprisingly the Post Office began to lose business to the new service—even though the law forbade the carrying of letters by any public servant other than an officer of the royal mail. People simply sent their letters in parcels by coach. Numerous postmasters in various parts of the country were experimenting with faster and safer systems, but it was John Palmer, postmaster at Bath, and faced with the most immediate threat, who produced the solution. Thanks to the advocacy of the young Prime Minister William Pitt this was taken up, and by the end of the century it had provided England with the fastest and most reliable postal service in the world. Here was another important factor that contributed to the rapid increase in England's power as an industrial and trading nation.

Palmer's scheme was practical. Rather than rival the coach service with some completely new technique (some postmasters were experimenting with light one-horse carts), he employed the stage-coach principle to hasten the mails. He proposed that contractors should run and maintain horse coaches able to carry the mail, four inside passengers and an armed guard; the contractors should be paid no more than the standard mileage rate allowed for the riding post but they should be free to make a profit on the passengers carried. By prohibiting the mail coach from carrying outside passengers and by removing the various roof furniture normally required for them he hoped to lighten the mail coach sufficiently to improve on the journey time of his rivals. He succeeded triumphantly on the trial run between Bristol and London which he organised, at his own expense, in August 1784. Palmer's mail coach knocked an hour off the up journey time and maintained this gain on the return journey.

Mail-coach services were rapidly set up on the major routes travelled by the royal mail, and by 1800 they were general. With only four passengers inside and none 'up' the fare was naturally high, but for those who could afford it the speed and the reliability were well worth while. It was, in effect, the equivalent of the express and Pullman service on the modern railway, and the phrase 'as regular as the mail' became a common simile.

The wear and tear on the coaches and the struggle to keep to tight schedules on roads that could barely cope with the slower stage-coach times soon threatened the service, however. Within ten years of its inauguration, an improved coach design had become standard on the mail routes and the most rigorous standards of vehicle maintenance were enforced by the Post Office authorities. The same high-quality check was also imposed on the grooming and care of the horses and, indeed, on every aspect of the immensely complicated business of running a nation-wide and reliable posting system. Despite much opposition from guards and drivers, the Post Office required each coach to carry a locked time-piece which could be opened for rewinding and regulating only by certain officials, while the time officially allowed for a change of horses was no more than five minutes. But fast and efficient road travel was a great novelty, and the contractors' business depended on keeping to the Post Office schedules so that both pride in rivalry between the ostlers at the different staging posts and the spur of business self-interest combined to reduce this time to less than two minutes in the most efficient establishments.

The coaching era

The glamour which still surrounds the memory of the coaching era is not the fiction of a later age. The speeds achieved were remarkable to contemporaries. When Telford's new London-to-Holyhead road was opened, the actual travelling time allowed for the 261 miles, exclusive of changes and meals, was just over twenty-three hours. But it was not only a matter of speed. The coaches and their superb horses were a splendid sight. The livery of the mail coach was a restrained but sumptuous combination of red, maroon and black, boldly picked out with the royal arms and the stars of the four orders of chivalry (*see* Plate 3). In contrast, the stage coaches were flamboyant, a gaudy and dazzling display of colour, decorated with the signs of the inns on which they were based, the name of the proprietor and often the name of the coach itself. Contemporary parallels are the proudly named and vividly painted buses and lorries of Nigeria or the West Indian countries.

At the heart of all this extroverted display was the very art of the coach drivers themselves, the technique of driving 'four in hand'. As late as the mid-eighteenth century a team of four horses was managed by a driver on the box who held the reins on one of the two forward horses. But by the beginning of the mail-coach era the demanding art of driving all four had been mastered and was the proudly kept trade secret of the coachmen. Yet it also fascinated their passengers and appealed, above all, to the sporting taste of many a young aristocrat. It was not unusual for a rich young nobleman to bribe the coach driver for a chance to practise his expertise with the team of a stage coach, and soon four-in-hand clubs sprang up, using specially light coaches, to provide all the trappings of what was in effect a new and highly popular sport.

The coaching era was to contemporaries, and has remained to posterity, one of the most brilliant and thrilling periods in the history of the English road. During its brief forty years or so of life it brought glamour and colour to the English landscape; it also provided a vitally needed service for the rapidly expanding commercial and industrial world and a new concept of punctuality in business dealings. All in all it set a high example for the railway companies which were to provide the 'high-fliers' of a new age.

In the following chapter we note some of the speeds that could be made on the best roads in continental Europe. On the *chaussées* of southern Germany or France up to eighty miles a day could be kept up over long distances but we should remember that such speeds were possible only between major centres. In France, which boasted the most advanced road system in Europe, anyone travelling from Paris to great provincial cities such as Lyons or Orléans could rely on a good road all the way, but the journey from Lyons to Orléans would be a very different and much more tedious matter. It is therefore worth noting that despite the generally appalling conditions in Britain, comparable and indeed better speeds could be put up over reasonable distances, even between the lesser provincial towns.

On the roads in England

In the 1770s a clergyman, who was obviously somewhat better off than the general run of parish clergy, paid four guineas for the hire of a 'postshay' to take him the ninety-odd miles from Oxford to Castle Cary in Somersetshire. He took care not to travel during the winter months, but, nevertheless, the fact that he could cover the distance within the day is impressive and demonstrates that, for all their shortcomings, the turn-pike trusts had brought improvements to the roads of England. Indeed, lest we be too easily swayed by the innumerable tales of hardship from eighteenth-century English travellers—tales common enough among travellers of all places and periods—it is salutary to listen to the views of some contemporaries who certainly believed that road improvements had changed the English scene during their lifetime.

In 1788 William Wilberforce, the member of parliament for Hull and the great opponent of the slave trade, was forced to leave London for a few months for health reasons. Dismayed at the number of other visitors at what he had hoped would be a peaceful rural retreat, he somewhat petulantly observed that 'the banks of the Thames are scarcely more public than those of Windermere'. We can take more seriously the observations of Arthur Young, writing in 1771. For him the flight from the countryside to the towns, which accompanied the beginnings of the Industrial Revolution, was much connected with the improvements in the roads brought about by the turnpikes. Better roads opened up new markets and changed the general pattern of living, enabling city-dwellers to live farther out of town and country folk to reach the cities much more easily. Above all, Young complained that London, which Cobbett was later to dub that great 'wen', was more accessible than it had been. Formerly the capital had remained a city of mystery and travellers' tales. 'But now,' wrote Young, with perhaps some exaggeration, 'a country fellow, one hundred miles from London, jumps on a coach box in the morning and for eight or ten shillings gets to Town by night.'

Highwaymen and rebels

Actually, as the wide-eyed rustic must have found on many an occasion, travelling to London was not always so simple. During most of the eighteenth century the odds of the coach being held up on the road were barely even. The danger in fact increased as one approached London for, within a twenty-mile radius of the centre, highwaymen and robbers of all kinds were particularly active.

This was hardly a novel situation. Edward I had ordered the clearing of 200-foot swathes on either side of roads to remove the cover for lurking criminals; his grandson Edward III had repeated the injunction with particular reference to the approaches to London. In the seventeenth century the profession of common robber had been dignified by the addition to its ranks of a number of gentlemen impoverished by the Civil War. Taking a lead from their plight, many less well-born 'knights of the road' came to protest their gentle origins, claiming, though with less frequency as the memories of the Commonwealth receded, to be loyal subjects of the Stuarts. They would assert that they had been forced into their way of life by the confiscations of the Parliamentarians and protest that they robbed only men of known Republican sympathies.

This convenient romanticism did not touch the most remarkable of England's road robbers during the seventeenth century. This was Mary Frith, known as Moll Cutpurse, who, at her death at the age of seventy-five in 1659, had amassed a large fortune and was something of a public figure. Middleton and Dekker's play on the career of Mary Frith, called *The Roaring Girle*, antedates by more than a century the most famous of all 'Newgate pastorals', *The Beggars' Opera*, which was performed before packed houses for one hundred nights in 1727, two years after the death of Jonathan Wild. Both these immensely successful works exploited the air of romantic fascination with which the English continued to regard their criminal classes well into the nineteenth century. The recent film based on the Great Train Robbery is part of a long tradition.

As may be imagined, the highwaymen, many of whom were ruffians, delighting in brutality, killing, burning or raping, played up to the part expected of them. The regular public hangings of these pretentious bandits, some of whom claimed the social virtues of the semi-legendary Robin Hood, were display pieces of phony heroics in which the thief played the part of the dashing adventurer, joking with the hangman and ignoring the priest. The crowds loved it: ladies swooned away in pity for those noble hearts brought so low, and men fought for possession of the corpses,

believed to have magical powers. Passions now largely confined to the
unsolicited mail of the Home Office were given full, free and public rein.

The idea of capital punishment as a deterrent was never more in vogue
than in the eighteenth century—the 'age of Reason' and such delicate
diversions as public death—and will never be more fully discredited. If
the traveller's brains were not spilled by a bullet from Dick Turpin, his
stomach was liable to be turned at every crossroads and vantage point
along the road by the sight of decaying and putrescent corpses of highwaymen, many in 'ingeniously made' iron cages, hanging from the public
gibbets. As a deterrent these were totally ineffective; yet they did have
their uses. Particularly valuable was the help they afforded to writers of
guide-books, one of which contains numerous directions of the 'first-
left-past-the-second-gibbet' type. Nor were the highwaymen slow to
appreciate the merits of these unmistakable landmarks; many a robbery
is recorded as having taken place in the shadow of a gibbet.

Nevertheless fact and romantic fiction did occasionally meet. The
highwaymen themselves seem to have been overcome with admiration of
their own reputation, disdaining to take any serious precautions against
capture and sticking to the well-worn routine of the black mask, the
fast horse and the levelled pistol. Whenever the authorities did find it in
their hearts to spend a few hundred pounds on crime prevention the
officers had little difficulty in taking the criminals. In the twelve years
between 1759 and 1771, two hundred and fifty highwaymen were hanged
at Tyburn alone.

The profession did have its occupational hazards, therefore, but it
also demanded a high level of 'social' accomplishment from its more
serious devotees. Some were, as they claimed, petty nobles come down in
the world; others were sons of clergymen (one was a Quaker) and, as
befitted such gentle folk, they demanded money with great civility—
unless they were crossed, in which case they usually took a life or two.
Wise travellers carried a second purse for the 'collectors', as the charming
euphemism had it, and many foreign visitors to England, used to less
mannerly thugs, expressed astonishment not only at the immense number of thieves at large on the king's highway but also at their charming and
courtly ways, especially with the ladies.

Undoubtedly, English roads were more plagued with robbers than
those of other countries. This was partly due to the tolerance shown by
the authorities towards inns that were the known resorts of criminals,
partly to the excellent cover provided by the hedgerows skirting most
English roads, but largely to the unwillingness of the people to tolerate
an effective police force and of the government to finance it. For a few
years London had an effective body of thief-catchers, thanks to the
efforts of the novelist and Justice, Henry Fielding, and his blind brother

John, but as soon as they had cleared the streets the government stopped their funds since there was, of course, now no crime wave. And the highwaymen did not always feel obliged to conduct their business on the exposed and inhospitable stretches of the open road; frequently they plied their trade in London. On one occasion King George II was held up and relieved of his purse while taking a stroll in the gardens of Kensington Palace. On another occasion a group of ladies attending a production at Sadler's Wells were assured by advertisement of the authorities that their return home to the elegant safety of Grosvenor Square would be protected by an armed horse patrol.

Whatever other thoughts may be provoked by a study of the history of English roads during the eighteenth century at least we may be led to doubt whether the Englishman's much-vaunted love of personal liberty is not quite simply a dislike of efficiency and a scarcely secret love of violence. The refusal to countenance the expenditure of public money on road-building, or on a central and effective police force, guaranteed him a road system that was among the least serviceable and the most dangerous in Europe.

7

Roads of Continental Europe

RENAISSANCE SCHOLARS IN Italy had shown a dilettante interest in the Roman techniques of road-building, but the first practical step towards a central control of roads by a major European government was the appointment of an intendant of coaches by Henry IV of France in 1594. Five years later he appointed a *Grand Voyer* with the responsibility for the main roads of France, while legal jurisdiction over the public roads was given to his great minister Sully. During the reign of his successor Louis XIII, Henry's moves towards centralisation were not followed up, but under the rule of his great son Louis XIV and his minister Colbert, roads occupied some place in the general pattern of state economic policy.

France, the cradle of modern road technology

The achievements of Louis XIV's reign were modest in the field of road-building. The real advances came during the eighteenth century, both in administration and design. In 1716, when the department of *Ponts et Chaussées* ('bridges and roads') was set up, France became the first European country with a government-appointed body charged exclusively with overseeing road transport. It is one of history's fitting coincidences that in this same year was born Pierre Trésaguet, who can reasonably be claimed as the founder of modern road technology.

Before Trésaguet's time, some of the basic principles of road-building, such as the need for good drainage, had sometimes been grasped though imperfectly applied, while the other basic principle, of economy, had been practised well beyond the limits of miserliness. A civil engineer was once described as a man who can 'do for one dollar what any damn fool can do for two', and the observation is sound enough, because it recognises that something at least must be done even if two dollars are needed. Civil engineering as applied to roads barely existed, and while on many occasions those concerned could be relied upon to spend one dollar where in fact two were needed, their money was frequently wasted. Trésaguet was one of the first to introduce the idea that road-building was susceptible to the operations of science. He designed pavements with two basic essentials: a firm, well-drained foundation, and a surface impervious to water. His roads consisted of three layers contained by large upright stones at either edge. The foundation was of large, heavy stones set on a cambered footing; above this came the 'base course' of somewhat smaller stones; and the surface was composed of small graded stones. Although flush with the surrounding topsoil, this was sure of adequate drainage because of its own cambered surface and the cambering of the levels beneath it.

France was the only country in which Trésaguet could have enjoyed an honourable and profitable career as a designer and builder of roads during the eighteenth century. In England, both Telford and McAdam achieved full recognition in this field only in the opening decades of the nineteenth, while their precursor, the famous Blind Jack of Knaresborough, despite his skill and fame, could never have hoped for the reputation of a professional man. From being deputy inspector of roads and municipal works in Paris, Trésaguet became chief civil engineer of Limoges, and finally inspector-general in 1775. He had already taken up his first appointment when in 1747 France opened the world's first officially recognised college of road engineering, the school of the department of *Ponts et Chaussées*. This was part of a developing pattern in which the government showed its active interest in the highways. In 1720 specifications were laid down for various types of road: the main routes were to be sixty feet in width with ditches of six feet, and the secondary routes thirty-six feet wide. The administrators also took account of the ancillary amenities and it was stipulated that new roads should be flanked by avenues of trees, spaced at thirty-foot intervals. By a further government regulation of 1776 four classes of road were specified, and both the materials to be used and the depths to be excavated were laid down.

The English traveller Arthur Young, whose observations on pre-Revolutionary France are so illuminating and valuable, was full of praise for her roads, and indeed along the main routes the advance was dramatic. The journey time from Paris to Lyons, some ten days in the seventeenth century, was cut in half in the eighteenth, and the road programme was taken so seriously that money was made available by the central exchequer, as well as by local taxes, to supplement the works undertaken by the *corvée* system of forced labour. At the centre of this great improvement scheme stood the Corps of Roads, Bridges and Highways, with a staff of more than two hundred and fifty engineers and inspectors, and a budget of more than 7 million *livres*. In 1786, three years before the great turmoil of the Revolution, the *corvée* had been replaced by a system of paid labour; the move was dictated by political considerations. Across the Channel, Englishmen looked in horror at the centralised and autocratic regime of France, to which disaster was soon to come, but there could be no doubt that in many practical matters it paid dividends.

By the year of the great Revolution and the collapse of the *Ancien Régime*, France had a more extensive and reliable system of trunk roads than any other country in Europe; however, crossroads between provincial towns and villages on the main routes out of Paris were still in the most primitive condition. Remembering de Tocqueville's observations on the importance of communications in the intellectual life of a nation, and remembering the speed with which news of events in Paris was circulated during the Revolution (and the events themselves sometimes imitated in the main provincial centres), one might suggest that the great improvement in French roads during the last fifty years of the Bourbon regime contributed, if only in a small degree, to its downfall.

Although French roads were technically advanced, travellers were certainly not free from the incidental hazards of robbery and murder, so common elsewhere. A particularly nasty story is found in contemporary news sheets for the year 1723. It records the fate of some Englishmen *en route* for Paris, possibly on the outward journey of their Grand Tour. On September 10 three gentlemen named Sebright, Davis and Mompesson, with their two servants, left the Silver Lion Inn at Calais for Boulogne. Before their departure, they had changed twenty-five English guineas into French money for the journey. Possibly the sight of so much money alerted the underworld network, for only a few miles outside Calais their two coaches were stopped by half a dozen mounted highwaymen. The English party, innocents abroad in the most literal sense, had no firearms and consequently were forced to give up all their money, about £130, their watches, jewels and, as a final insult, their swords. All five were then ordered to lie face down on the ground and, when they had been searched again, they were shot and viciously cut about by the robbers. Another Englishman travelling towards Calais drove straight into the affray and he, too, lost his life. Throughout the massacre the French coachmen made no attempt, probably wisely, at rescue, but the fact that despite a large reward offered by the French government only one man was ever arrested for the crime, suggests that the coachmen knew the culprits too well to risk informing on them.

Such wanton killing was not the rule, but there are numerous other instances, both in France and elsewhere, of extensive banditry on the highway, though it was nowhere so widespread as in England.

The upheavals caused by the Revolution affected roads as they did so many other aspects of domestic administrative policy. The Republican government soon imposed road taxes. These were so profitable that by the ninth year of the Republic they were yielding more than $10\frac{1}{2}$ million francs a year. However, they were usually diverted to other uses and the state of the highways was a subject of scandal and national concern. With the inauguration of the Empire matters improved, for the traveller if for no other section of the population. Later in this chapter we describe some of the mighty achievements of civil engineering that resulted from Napoleon's military ambitions, but of course they were possible only through the work of large gangs of navvies, and the cost had to be met somehow. In this mundane aspect of state affairs, as in so many others, the ambitious dictator aped the manners of his royal predecessors—forced labour was introduced and the *corvée*, one of the most hated symbols of royal oppression in the *Ancien Régime*, was resurrected, though with a new name. The French peasant, obliged, at the behest of the government, to leave his fields and work on the roads, so essential to the progress of the imperial armies, could at least tell himself that he was no longer labouring under the injustices of the *corvée*, abolished too late by a slothful royal government. Old men were familiar with the system; young men knew only the name and, compelled by the requirements of Napoleon's *prestation en nature*, worked for nothing.

Elsewhere in Europe

The comments of Arthur Young on the roads of France have been noted, but there were fine roads in some other parts of Europe. We have the evidence of that inveterate traveller James Boswell, who went about the business of meeting famous men in all weathers and all conditions, as to the comparative ease of journeying in such countries as Switzerland even in the depth of winter. He notes for 20 December 1764, 'I had sad roads to Lausanne,' but two weeks earlier on his way from Berne to Brot he records 'a fine hard road amidst mountains covered with snow'. For an Englishman a good road in the heart of winter was indeed worthy of remark and, during the eighteenth century, a number of the mountain roads in Switzerland were well maintained; in the year 1793 the German writer Reichard, whose *Guide for Travellers* was a worthy forerunner of Baedeker, tells his readers that the main roads between Switzerland and Italy were, almost without exception, well metalled and carried food and regular post services.

In general it would appear that conditions were better for the traveller

in Switzerland and southern Germany. Reichard also notes that the roads
serving the main routes south from Frankfurt or Nuremberg to Vienna
and thence to Switzerland were all excellent; after them he praised the
quality of roads in Bavaria and the Palatinate. One of the most pleasant
roads in this part of Germany was that from the famous university town
of Heidelberg in the Palatinate to the town of Darmstadt, about thirty
miles due north. Even in this short distance the road passed through
the territories of three separate governments. Leaving the lands of the
Elector Palatine, it traversed part of the bishopric of Mainz for a distance
of some seven miles before crossing the border into the Landgravate
of Hesse-Darmstadt. When we remember that by the late eighteenth
century the German lands had become divided between no fewer than
three hundred rulers and independent towns, it is not difficult to imagine
the problems of building trunk roads over any significant distance.
Nevertheless, the Bergstrasse, as it was called, between Heidelberg and
Darmstadt was praised not only by Reichard but also by English travellers
on the Grand Tour.

In the political conditions of the Germany of the time good roads could
only be built in the relatively larger states, or in states where the absolute
ruler felt the necessity for them. Following the French example the state
of Hesse had begun a programme of metalled roads or '*chaussées*' as early
as 1720, and over the next fifty years the states of Baden and Württemberg
took similar action. In the north, despite the power and the size of
Prussia, conditions were very much worse. This was to be explained
partly by the lack of good building stone, but also, no doubt, by the fact
that the Prussian state, for all its size, was not rich, and devoted much of
its energies to the building of its armies and the ambitions and aggressive
wars of conquest.

Conditions in northern Germany must indeed have made even an
Englishman grateful for the efforts of the turnpike trusts at home.
Reichard warns that during the rainy months of the year the traveller
might find himself obliged to leave the 'road' for a cross-country route
over less-traversed fields and byways. Since ruts were so deep and so
permanent, even their gauges were an important consideration. He advised
against the use of one's own carriage, unless its track could be adjusted,
since the rut-gauge differed from one part of the country to another,
according to the standard tracks of local wagons and carriages. As far as
its overland transport was concerned the Germany of Frederick the Great
suffered in comparison with neolithic Malta—there the rut-ways were at
least adapted to a standard gauge. As late as the 1840s an English traveller
in the Harz mountains described roads where the carriage might sink
down to its axles in the ruts, and where the mud churned up by the
passage of innumerable heavy vehicles stood up like walls in the road.

In such conditions it is remarkable that any serious traffic made use of Germany's roads. But of course the instances quoted, although not uncommon, represent only part of the story. Generally the roads seem to have been sufficiently good to make an average daily journey of about twenty miles possible—about the same as the speed over non-turnpike roads in England. In addition to the private traffic, there was also a fairly extensive system of public coaches, though these were not up to the standards of interior comfort that passengers could expect on an English stage coach.

All except the very wealthy shared their journey with others, whether on the public service or in a privately hired coach. Boswell tells us how, on journeying to Berlin in the *jounalière* or daily public coach, 'he spoke words of German to a lass called Mademoiselle Dionisius', who turned out to be the daughter of the cook to Prince Ferdinand of Prussia. Later in the same month of July 1764 he hired a coach and was able to give three German gentlemen a lift (presumably they contributed to the fare) to Charlottenburg in Prussia. Another Englishman, Crabb Robinson, making the journey from Hamburg to Frankfurt, a distance of 315 miles, shared a coach with three fellow-travellers, and although they were joined by another four along the route, Robinson found himself charged £7 8s. 0d. for the fare. At prices then current such a charge was exorbitant and thereafter Robinson preferred to walk.

The idea of a gentleman walking for preference was astonishing at a time when pedestrian traffic on Germany's roads was confined to the poorer classes, among them journeymen craftsmen on their *Wanderjahre*. Most younger men of any means would expect to travel on horseback, and all travellers would hope to be able to lodge with friends along their journey. Germany boasted few roadside inns that could compare with the hostelries of eighteenth-century England, and for the most part the tourist or businessman could expect to spend the night on a palliasse of straw on the floor of the main public room. But the situation was better in the big hotels of the main towns, and particularly in important commercial centres such as Frankfurt.

But if road travel was both expensive and fraught with discomfort in northern Germany, on the best *chaussées* in the south distances of up to sixty miles a day could be achieved by a well-found coach or post-chaise, and over the whole region the main roads were well provided with posthouses offering a change of horses every ten or fifteen miles. Throughout the century, moreover, there was an efficient letter post carried, as in England, either on regular coach services or by horsemen. As early as the beginning of the seventeenth century, when the authority of the German emperor was still more than merely nominal, a monopoly had been granted to a company to carry the mails of the whole empire. Although, as the independence of the many small princes became confirmed, its territory was diminished, it was still running at the end of the eighteenth century, employing as many as 20,000 staff, and making a respectable annual profit. In 1800 letters took about seven days to get from Frankfurt to Vienna—some fifty-two miles a day. This was among the better times then recorded for the German posts but it did not begin to approach the speeds established sixteen years before on the English mail-coach service. Still more significant, the punctuality, on the English scale, was still a thing of the future in Germany, as in other Continental countries.

Road-building in the Alps

The great barriers of world geography have always proved a challenge to road-makers, and have often given rise to some of the finest achievements in engineering. No single part of the earth's surface is more rich in these great undertakings than the Alpine range in Europe, where since the beginning of the nineteenth century each new generation has produced some further marvel of man's ingenuity in the face of overwhelming odds.

The first great classic was the forcing of the Simplon pass. The Romans had made use of the route and had driven a road through, but their work had fallen into decay and the pass had carried only intermittent traffic during the Middle Ages. It regained new importance in the seventeenth century when the Swiss merchant Gaspard de Stockalper built his fortune on the trade between Switzerland and Italy, and developed the route intensively through his monopolistic control of the mule trains and cara-vans between Milan and Lausanne. The monument to Stockalper's prosperity, the towered castle that he built for himself overlooking the road at Brig, still stands, but the road that earned him his wealth was not to come into the forefront of European affairs until another century had passed.

This time the traffic was of a different kind. Soldiers started up the punishing ascent through the Saltina ravine to the lofty pass. They were under the command of General Bethencourt, and, as members of the pioneer corps of the army of Napoleon, were charged with finding an easier crossing into Italy than the great St Bernard pass that the French commander had used on his way across the Alps to the great victory of Marengo. Despite the hardships of the crossing he had led an army of 30,000 men from France into Italy, but now he was determined to find better lines of communication. With his characteristic eye for country, Napoleon was convinced that an easier way would be found in the Simplon region. He ordered his surveyors to discover a route suitable for the trans-port of the artillery train of the *Grande Armée*. But there were problems of terrain, leadership and administration; it was not until a task force of

6,000 men, under the command of the great civil engineer Céard, set to work that the road began to make progress. Then the rate of advance was indeed remarkable; the road was completed in five short summers, the only months when work was possible, and was opened to traffic in the year 1805. From Lake Geneva to Lake Maggiore it had cost an average of 12 million francs per mile; the distance as the crow flies is only five miles but the specifications called for an average gradient of 1:30. The steepest gradient is only 1:11 and the total length of the road is nearer twenty miles. The cost in lives has been estimated at somewhere between four hundred and seven hundred deaths; the working conditions were appalling.

In the astonishing Gondo gorge, where in places the cliffs rise sheer to a height of 3,000 feet, the road makes its way like the thread of some crazed spider, through galleries hewn out of the rock face high above the foaming Diveria river, leaping from side to side across bridges that are miracles of engineering. Explosives were used but every shot-hole had to be bored by hand with long, cumbersome drills, and the charges had to be fired with burning fuses which were often damp and dangerously un-reliable. Many a life was lost as men were ordered forward to examine the state of a fuse long overdue but in fact still live; at other times the ropes carrying the work cradles broke, sending men to their death on the rocks below. Throughout the tremendous operation life was in constant jeopardy from rock slips and landslides. Constructions such as the bridge at Saltina survive as monuments to heroic achievement, but above all it is the road itself that is a continuing witness to the workers' courage and skill. The modern Swiss engineer Franz Wallack, himself responsible for another magnificent Alpine road, the Grossglocknerstrasse, has said that the con-struction of the Simplon road would be a major undertaking even given all the advantages of modern equipment, and regards it as the model of all subsequent Alpine roads. By the middle of the nineteenth century it had become one of the marvels of Europe, and the regular coach service across it was used as much be sightseers as by travellers, one of the most famous descriptions being by Charles Dickens in his *Travels in Italy*.

Later in the nineteenth century the route was to be provided with protection against the danger of falling rocks and landslips from above, when the engineer Venetz constructed the famous galleries, with their arched windows overlooking the gorge. Other monuments to the heroic days of earlier ages, when the traveller who journeyed for pleasure was a rarity, are the hospices, found on many of the Alpine routes, among them the Stockalper and Napoleon Hospice. Even today, conditions for the Alpine traveller can be both arduous and dangerous; hotels on the longer routes are welcome resting places in the middle of a strenuous drive, while it is still found necessary on occasion to protect the most modern motor roads from the hazards of landslides.

Not since the time of the Romans had there been such a classic example of military influence on road-building as that offered by Napoleon. Indeed, the value that he placed on good communications was so high that between the years 1804, when he was proclaimed emperor, and 1812, the year of the invasion of Russia, he is estimated to have spent twice as much money on roads as on the building of fortifications. His activities in the Alps were not confined to the Simplon pass; he also spent 20 million francs on a road over the Mont Cenis pass, completed in 1810 (*see* Plate 10). Shortly after it was opened the road was carrying as many as 14,000 goods wagons and 3,000 passengers a year. The approach roads to it were improved, and the ancient Roman Via Aurelia in Italy was modernised. In France itself, he did much to continue the growing tradition of state road-building, and the modern motorist, familiar with the long, straight, poplar-lined roads of northern France, can appreciate the intelligent attention to detail with which the military engineers of the *Grande Armée* took care to protect the long columns of marching troops from the heat of the sun.

In the fatal days of 1814, when the imperial armies were shattered after the battle of Leipzig, both the Simplon and the Mont Cenis were in enemy hands, but there remained one route of communication across the Alps. This was the southerly pass known as Mont Genèvre, over the Cottian Alps. The route was well known to the Romans, being much used by travellers to Gaul. Along this, Julius Caesar had once made the journey from Rome to Geneva in eight days, while it was here that the army of the French king Charles VIII had crossed into Italy with no fewer than six hundred pieces of ordnance in 1494. The pass is nothing like so daunting as those so far mentioned, but nevertheless in 1802 Napoleon had had the foresight to commission the building of a new military road which had been completed in 1807.

The improvement of Alpine communications during the nineteenth century was by no means left entirely to the great French conqueror, however. In the 1820s a new road was built over the Splugen which, fifty years after its completion in 1882, was carrying passenger traffic at the rate of 20,000 people a year. Like so many other Alpine roads this is a tourist attraction as well as a trunk route, thanks to the fact that it bridges the Via Mala, one of the wildest and most picturesque gorges in Switzerland. The pass had been in use since the Middle Ages, and in the last quarter of the fifteenth century one of the earliest of the Alpine roads was built here, thanks to the co-operation of the neighbouring Swiss cantons. It remained one of the major points of passage across the Alps until the driving of a rail tunnel, during the later nineteenth century, robbed it, like so many of the other Alpine road routes, of much of their traffic. Following the coming of the motor-car these roads are once more jammed with vehicles.

As the industrial revolution gathered momentum in Europe, communications of all kinds became more and more vital, and many of the lesser Alpine passes achieved their first metalled roads. One of these was the Lukmanier between Disentis and Olivone. A much-used route since the early Middle Ages, it boasted a monastic hospice to St Sigisbert which was built as early as the year 700. It was used also by Charlemagne on his journeys into Italy, and may well have served the party of raiding Saracens, lodged in the Italian Alps, who burst into the Rhine valley in the mid-tenth century. More hospices were built in the Middle Ages and the Emperor Barbarossa, following the example of his illustrious predecessor, favoured this road. But in the thirteenth century its popularity declined in favour of the newly opened route over the St Gotthard (*see* Plate 11), and it was not until the 1870s that a new road was built. Like many others in the region this has features that make it a remarkable feat of engineering: in one section a series of ten tunnels was driven through the mountain range in the course of a rise of some 800 feet. Indeed, one of the few Alpine routes without some such distinguishing feature is the road, built in 1772, over the historic Brenner pass.

The railways conquered the roads even in the seemingly unfavourable terrain of the Alps. The historic achievements of their builders cannot be told here, but such works as the Brig–Isella tunnel which took the railway under the Simplon and the St Gotthard rail tunnel, opened in 1882, threatened the whole *raison d'être* of the Alpine roads. Until that year traffic over the St Gotthard had amounted to nearly 70,000 passengers per year, but it quickly lost business to the new mode of transport. Its popularity had risen sharply since the thirteenth century and, as we have seen, a bridge was built over the Schollenen gorge in the Middle Ages, but it had remained exclusively a route for pack animals until the 1770s. On one or two subsequent occasions Goethe used the pass on his way to Italy.

The present road was built during the 1820s, and it links Lake Lucerne with Lake Lugano. The ascent begins at the town of Altdorf on the northern side of the pass, and from here to the summit road is a distance of thirty-three miles; the real ascent is somewhat over a mile. From the summit of the pass to the town of Bellinzona to the south, the road drops 6,200 feet in forty-nine miles so that the total distance traversed by the road is eighty-two miles, although the distance between the two points 'as the crow flies' is almost exactly fifty miles. Overall the average gradient is about 1:30, while the steepest stretches are no more than 1:10; to cope with the steep rise in altitude, and maintain the average gradient, the road twists and turns back on itself, and on the southern side at Cantoniera Val Tremola there are no fewer than forty-eight hairpin bends.

8

Roads in America up to 1900

THE 'ROADS' USED by the Indians who inhabited North America before the coming of the white man were trails blazed through wooded country and marked through the open plains by familiar landmarks. Blazing a trail consisted of clearing a route 'surveyed' by the scouts, and marking it by stripping sections of bark from trees and by using other signs handed down in traditional wood-lore. Many of these trails were of great length, particularly those in the vast territory controlled by the Iroquois Confederacy which, by the end of the seventeenth century, was bounded by the Ottawa river in the north, the Illinois to the west and the Tennessee to the south.

In the north, the Mohawk trail ran up the valley of the Mohawk river, the largest of the tributaries of the Hudson, to Niagara falls, crossing the area south of Lake Ontario. It provided the easiest route through the mountain chain from New York State, and was used by thousands of settlers in their trek westwards; during the eighteenth century it was improved by a number of turnpikes, and remained in active use until the early decades of the nineteenth century when the opening of the Erie canal and the coming of the railways reduced its value as a freighting route.

Other famous Indian trails were the Old Connecticut path, from the upper valley of the Hudson river near Albany to the Atlantic coast near Boston; the Nemacolin trail, blazed in the mid-eighteenth century by Nemacolin, the chief of the Delaware Indians, and Thomas Cresap, a Maryland frontiersman, westward from the Potomac river; and finally the great Natchez trace. Technically these trails were primitive, but the routes they opened up often proved the best available through the country, and were used by successive generations of white Americans who widened and improved them for their own purposes.

In the case of the Natchez trace the work of the Indian 'surveyors' is commemorated today by an expressway built along a route substantially unchanged. The trace was in fact a series of Indian trails running from Natchez, Mississippi, to Nashville, Tennessee, a distance of about 450 miles, and was traversed with increasing frequency during the eighteenth century by the French, English and Spanish colonists. At first it was used by them only in the northerly direction, since flat boats operating on the Cumberland and Mississippi could take passengers and freight all the way down from Nashville to New Orleans; but, as the United States continued its expansion into the south-west, the road was utilised in both directions and in 1800 became a post road. Later Andrew Jackson marched along it to New Orleans in the War of 1812 but, when steam navigation became general on the Mississippi, it fell into disuse.

The history of American road-building really begins with the British general Edward Braddock, a man who had little military experience but was 'strong on discipline'. He arrived as commander of the king's forces in North America in February 1755. His first objective was the capture of the French base of Fort Duquesne, at the Ohio Forks across the Allegheny. Starting from Fort Cumberland (the modern town of Cumberland, Maryland), with the bulky baggage train that his training in European tactics made obligatory, he had, perforce, to build a road as he went. The campaign ended in disaster and with the death of Braddock, despite some sound advice from his aide-de-camp, the twenty-three-year-old Major George Washington. The road was of more lasting value and formed the basis of the future National Road.

Another famous route of the pre-Independence era was the Wilderness road, opened up by that renowed frontiersman Daniel Boone, which ran from Virginia south-west through the Cumberland gap. Boone had himself probably served as a wagoner in Braddock's ill-fated expedition, and he may have learnt something of the business of road-building from the work of the army engineers. But when, in 1775, he undertook to open a trail into Kentucky for the Transylvania company, his immediate problem was the hostility of the local Indian tribes. Accompanied by a small band of armed men, and following for part of the route a succession of old Indian trails, known collectively as the Warrior's Path, Boone reached the Kentucky river, and founded the town of Boonesboro. For fifty years this road was one of the important routes for westward migrations, though the danger from hostile Indians remained severe until the early years of the nineteenth century. Only after Kentucky had become a state in the 1790s was the road made passable for wheeled traffic; even then it was a difficult journey and certain stretches were handed over to toll companies to improve and maintain.

The age of turnpikes

In the matter of road-building the colonial government followed the policy of the mother country and did nothing. The inheritance of the new nation was limited to the Cumberland road laid out by Braddock. Americans of the colonial period were probably familiar with the principle of the turnpike from English example, but the first American turnpike was a state enterprise launched by Virginia. This was opened only in 1785 and it was not until the 1790s, when private companies began to operate, that the movement gathered strength.

In 1794 the Philadelphia–Lancaster turnpike opened; it had an overall width of thirty-seven feet, a stone and gravel surface twenty-four feet wide and was the first major paved road in North America. Serving a prosperous agricultural region, it rapidly showed considerable profits, and was able to give dividends to shareholders of as much as 15 per cent.

By the mid 1820s such roads with their toll-gates were a common sight all over the eastern states. Among the better-known were the roads from Boston to New York, from New York to Albany, one on either side of the Hudson river, and the roads westward from Albany to Buffalo. The great period of the turnpikes was the first forty years of the century, and the traffic that used them ranged from stage coaches to droves of horses, sheep and cattle. Many settlers too, moving west, were sped on the first stage of their journey over such excellent routes.

During their heyday the turnpikes amply repaid the expenses of their building. Toll-gates at intervals of between six and ten miles levied rates of up to 25 cents per vehicle so that, for example, to travel the whole length of the Lancaster pike through its nine gates might cost a wagoner as much as $2.25. But the service was well worth the charge as generally these roads were well built and maintained. Since large stretches ran through wooded country, the first operation was to clear the ground, felling the trees and grubbing the stumps; after this the surface was levelled and, in marshy places, a corduroy road-bed of logs laid down in layers. The road surface proper might be of beaten earth, but more often consisted of planks or broken stones. The cost ranged from $5,000 to $10,000 per mile. With the development of the canal, and above all the railway network, they rapidly lost custom. In the second half of the century more and more companies wound up their affairs and handed over their responsibilities to the various state governments.

One of the few important roads built in America at this time was that between Fort Benton, the head of navigation on the Missouri, and Fort Walla Walla in Washington State, a distance of about 400 miles. Known as the Mullan Wagon road after its engineer John Mullan, it was completed in 1863. The original purpose was military, but later it was used by civilians and, after extensive renovations in the 1860s, it was important in opening up the north-west territories to miners and settlers.

The first, and for more than a century the only, federally financed highway project was the National Road. Public demand for a new road to the west had been building up since the beginning of the century, and in 1806 Congress voted funds for the preliminary surveys. The first stretch was to run for the most part over General Braddock's Cumberland road, which in its turn had made use of the Nemacolin path. Building did not start until 1811 and, due to delays caused by the war with Britain, only twenty miles had been completed by the end of the following year. Thereafter matters progressed more rapidly, and within six years it had advanced a further eighty miles to Wheeling, by the east bank of the Ohio river. The funds for the initial stretch had been raised by the sale of public lands in Ohio which, on becoming a state, had in 1803 guaranteed not to tax such lands for the first five years. In fact the road reached Columbus, Ohio, in 1833. In its first stretch out of Wheeling it followed an earlier route, the famous trace to Maysville in Kentucky, pioneered by Ebenezer Zane. After 1838 Congressional funds for the extension of the road ceased and, to maintain it, toll-gates were set up and responsibility accepted by the states. The National Road, which eventually reached as far west as St Louis, is still commemorated by the modern U.S. Highway 40, and the memory of its importance as a pioneering route is kept alive by little statues known as 'Madonnas of the Trail', erected at points along the road in honour of the women who took part in the early pioneer migrations.

With the improvement of the roads went improvement in the postal services. In the eastern states these relied on the stage coaches, which could reach remarkable speeds; record runs averaging fifteen miles an hour over a twenty-mile stretch were recorded, while the coach messenger carrying the news of the declaration of war against Mexico in 1842 achieved over 130 miles in twelve hours. Such average times were well up to the best that was achieved by the English Post Office during the mail-coach era, and were to be equalled by the brief, but heroic, achievements of the pony express.

The first telegraph line had been set up in 1844, and by 1860 the telegraph had reached as far west as St Joseph, Missouri. In April of that year began one of the most remarkable postal services the world has ever seen. The pony express from St Joseph to Sacramento in California operated a weekly service over a distance of 2,000 miles, much of it through hostile Indian territory and all of it over appallingly bad roads. Stages were set up every ten to fifteen miles, and the entire distance was covered in eight days. In October 1861 the telegraph reached San Francisco and thereafter the express was discontinued, but despite its brief life its achievements rapidly became part of the legend of the west.

The westering trails

Thanks to the glossy celluloid of Hollywood's Wild West and the memory of the sensational gold rushes, the ruthless epic of nineteenth-century America's pioneering drive to the Pacific is now a part of the world's folk memory. 'Cowboys and Indians', and the doughty battles of sheriffs and badmen, are the centre of the myth, but the arduous trek of the wagon trains, struggling across the great American desert in search of profit and adventure, in that order, was at the heart of the reality (*see* Plate 13). Their enemies were the vast and inhospitable open spaces of an untamed continent, and the violent rearguard action of the native Indians fighting to preserve their ancient way of life. The first destination of the wagon-masters was the town, then Mexican, of Santa Fé.

As the century progressed, commerce had new objectives in the pioneer towns of the developing states that flanked the Union to north and west, and without the yearly trips of the prairie schooners these communities would have remained primitive backwaters. In the 1860s the driving of the railroad from the East Coast to the Pacific killed the long-distance wagon trade, but it is doubtful whether the railway would have been built so early had not the wagoners enabled the new towns to grow into healthy new communities of consumers ripe for the exploitation of eastern commerce.

Here, there is only space for an outline account of the trade which, in the half-century between the 1810s and the coming of the railway, grew up across North America. It is, however, an essential part of our story for it shows how the conditions of the terrain and the nature of the traffic compelled these nineteenth-century merchants to strike out along trails that had all the hallmarks of the earliest roads used by man.

The Santa Fé trail and the development of freighting

The town of Santa Fé was established by the Spanish at the beginning of the seventeenth century. Founded as an advance post of Spanish missionary activity among the Indians (hence the name), it had been supplied since the earliest days by wagon train from distant Mexico City, and there was also an overland link, evolved later, with Los Angeles. In the year 1609 the Spanish government of Mexico laid plans for a regular three-yearly wagon train consisting of thirty-two wagons, each of two-ton capacity, with an escort of some fifteen soldiers. Historically the earliest long-distance freighting service on the North American continent, the train was intended to carry only necessary supplies for the mission post. But inevitably, as time went on, commercial trade developed and Santa Fé became an important centre for trade with the local Indian population. The business was controlled by the merchants of the town of Chihuahua, some 500 miles south of Santa Fé on the direct route to Mexico, and it seems that they were content to use the northern entrepôt as a dumping ground for their second-quality goods.

Even before Mexico won its independence from Spain in 1821, there had been some slight contact between Santa Fé and American fur traders. But in the year of independence these contacts took on a new dimension when William Becknell, on his way to trade with the Comanche Indians, was persuaded to divert to Santa Fé by a party of Mexican soldiers. The results were highly profitable. Becknell, sizing up the situation and realising the possibilities for a merchant with first-class goods, returned the next year with a train of three wagons loaded with the best-quality goods he could find.

Becknell's base of operations was in Missouri, and the potentialities of the new route were rapidly appreciated by the Missouri senator Thomas Hart Benton. He had received a report from one of the merchants who had accompanied Becknell on a later expedition, and in 1825 he succeeded in getting a bill through Congress authorising the expenditure of $30,000 on surveying and marking the trail, and on the payment of compensation to tribes of Plains Indians. The surveyors largely failed in their commission, first because the markers they set up were simply piles of earth and turf and were quickly swept away by rains and storm, and secondly, because they did not bother to seek the help of the traders who had already been using the trail. Yet despite this, and the failure of the American and Mexican governments to come to an agreement on the policing of the trail, the trade flourished and grew rapidly.

The route started, initially, from the town of Franklin and, later, from Independence on the Missouri; thence it travelled 120 miles to the Arkansas river frontier with Mexico. The trail hit the Arkansas at the Great Bend, near the modern town of Larned, about 250 miles from Missouri. From here it followed the course of the river for about 100 miles until it came to the lowest of the crossings. Here the trail forked. One branch, known as the Cimarron Cutoff, headed across country direct for Santa Fé; the other, the Mountain Branch, followed the course of the river 150 miles westward. Each route had dangers, but the Mountain Branch could boast the only sign of civilisation on the long road from Missouri to Santa Fé; this was Bent's Fort, established in 1829 by William Bent and his brother from St Louis. It was a large place, requiring a staff of almost one hundred men, and its buildings included such refinements as a barber's shop and an icehouse, while the cooking was known far and wide. Much of the trade that passed through the fort headed north for the mines of Colorado, but merchants bound for Santa Fé who had made the long diversion, perhaps to link up with traders from Denver, or simply for the haven of the well-equipped fort, now struck south through the Raton mountains.

Here the going was so steep that in places the wagons had to be lowered down by ropes. During the 1860s the worst stretches of the route were improved, and a toll road established that yielded its builder 'Uncle' Richard Wootton, an old frontiersman, as much as $5,000 a year.

Nevertheless the Cimarron Cutoff, which crossed the Arkansas river about twenty miles west of Dodge City and ran for part of its length along

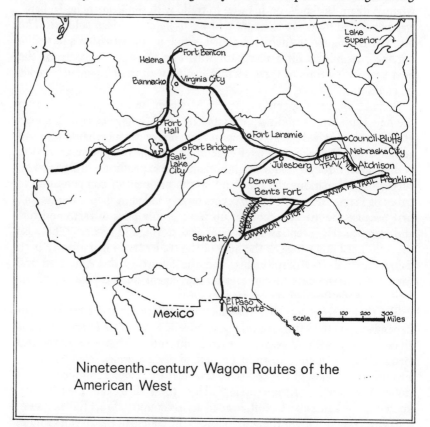

Nineteenth-century Wagon Routes of the American West

the valley of the Cimarron river, was preferred by most traders. Here the crossing of the Arkansas was the main hazard. The wide, shallow water-course was pitted with deep channels that forced the draught animals to swim a considerable distance, while at other places the bottom was treacherous with quicksands. To keep the wagons moving, as many as fifty yoke of oxen might be hitched up and when, on occasion, they stuck despite all efforts, the situation could only be saved by unloading in mid-stream and even dismantling the wagon which had to be man-handled piecemeal to the farther shore. But even after this ordeal was behind them the wagonmasters and their teams had to contend with long stretches of waterless desert. Here the deprivation was sometimes so acute that they would order camp a mile or more from the next water hole to avoid the possibility of a stampede when the beasts smelt water.

Other trails to the west

The Santa Fé trail was the first great wagon route and it was here that many famous entrepreneurs and wagonmasters did their apprenticeship, but as the move of westward migration gathered strength many new routes were worked. Chief among these was the Overland trail which gathered traffic from Kansas City, Leavenworth, Atchison and Omaha on the Missouri, and found a number of destinations to the west, such as Denver, Colorado; Helena, Montana; Oregon, California and Salt Lake City. Indeed, the Overland route in reality comprised a number of separate trails that shared the same course for part of their distance and then fanned out to their various destinations. Whereas the road to Santa Fé was, throughout its history, a commercial artery, the Overland routes were in the first instance used for migration. The main drive to the Far West began with the movement to Oregon in 1843 of some nine hundred farmers seeking new lands in the vast territory comprising the modern states of Washington, Idaho, Oregon and parts of Canada disputed between the American settlers and the British government. After the dispute was settled and the boundary fixed at the forty-ninth parallel in 1846, the 'Oregon' trail, first opened by the trappers of the Rocky mountains known as the mountain men, became increasingly busy. For the most part the routes out of Missouri followed the valleys of the north and south Platte rivers; farther west the trail divided, one route going north-west to the territory of Oregon, the other heading south-west to Salt Lake City and then still farther south to California.

The first train of emigrants reached California in 1841. The following year, another party, led by Elijah White, arrived in Oregon, but after the 'great' emigration the pace increased and in 1845 the total number of emigrants exceeded three thousand.

At about the same time another great migration was taking place, which ended with the settlement of the Mormons, driven out of Illinois by persecution, in Salt Lake City in 1847. Very soon after its founding, the industry of the Mormon settlement had raised the desert conditions of the Great Salt Lake valley to a state of high fertility, but the thriving community was desperately short of manufactured goods. Eastern traders were not slow to recognise the possibilities; the first 'merchant venture' was in the year 1849 and disposed of goods to the value of $20,000. By the following year four trading firms were established at Salt Lake City and were doing very well—a contemporary summed it up: '. . . the cry of the people is goods, Goods, GOODS.' The hardy wagoners carried cargoes of everything from ladies' bonnets to lemon syrup, from parasols to pepper, and in the 1860s an enterprising young trader was able to make a profit of between 400 and 500 per cent, by shipping kitchen stoves by wagon train over the 1,500-mile trail from Des Moines in Iowa to the numerous Mormon housewives. Toughness, enterprise and stiff religious ideals founded the colony in the Great Salt Lake basin, but without the wagon freighter the enterprise, like so many others that opened up the western part of the continent, would probably have foundered.

The prairie 'sea' and its ports

At the beginning of the nineteenth century the United States was confined to the eastern part of its present territory, despite the large acquisition of territory made by the Louisiana Purchase in 1803. The westward frontier was effectively formed by the Mississippi and Missouri rivers, and between these waterways and the Atlantic seaboard a great deal of the traffic was carried on navigable waterways, rivers and canals. An important improvement to the communications of this district was the Erie canal, from Buffalo on Lake Erie to the Hudson river, ten miles north of Albany. This was opened in 1825. More ambitious were works of the Pennsylvania canal, comprising long stretches of canal linked by inclined planes and portages, opened in 1834.

By 1840 a number of other canals had been constructed, among them those which linked the Lake Erie ports of Toledo, at the south-west corner, and Cleveland at the south-east corner and the towns of Cincinatti (due south of Toledo) and Portsmouth (due south of Cleveland) on the Ohio river. Other important communication links were the railways—the Baltimore–Ohio railroad, for example, linked Chesapeake Bay and the Ohio river and a number of watercourses between them; and there were of course a number of made roads in this prosperous eastern region. These we shall be dealing with later in this chapter; the point to be emphasised here is that the states to the east of the Missouri, which developed rapidly for historical reasons, were also blessed with a good network of inland waterways that were quickly improved by engineering works. Steamboats plied up the Mississippi from New Orleans as far north as St Paul in Minnesota, and the Mississippi trade could sail up the Ohio river and its tributaries to the heart of Pennsylvania and even as far north as New York State. Everywhere to the east of the Mississippi–Missouri, access was easy and also cheap by steamboat. At Nashville the coming of steam in 1818 cut the price of salt, the age-old measure of prices, from $3 per bushel to 75 cents.

To the west there were no such advantages. The river valleys formed an important part of the wagon routes but the rivers themselves were either too shallow or too treacherous. The Missouri, navigable for 3,000 miles upstream from St Louis, was unsatisfactory for two main reasons. First, its course lies too far northwards to serve the first routes of the westerly trade; secondly, in the upper reaches the river is too shallow for much of the year to be usable. The steamboat captains, who later came to open the trade to the north-west after the gold strike in Montana, had to contend with treacherous high and low water levels, ice during the winter, and the hazards of high winds sweeping off the prairie and threatening to run their vessels on to the banks. The river was also difficult farther south. The record run from St Louis to Omaha, a distance of 678 miles took 5 days and 15 hours, an average speed of almost exactly five miles an hour; by contrast steamers on the Mississippi could expect to average more than seven miles an hour. Nevertheless the head of navigation was gradually pushed farther north and west so that the overland trails were able to make contact with the river traffic at different points.

Of mules and men

From the Missouri, the cross-continental journey had to be continued by land, along one of the routes that we have described above. The wagon or prairie 'schooner' was used for all bulky loads, but on some trails and for some types of cargoes that were light but valuable the mule train was commonly used. Pack trains had been on the road since the beginning of the century and were always at an advantage in rough or unfamiliar terrain. But, apart from the fact that a beast could drag three times the weight it could carry, a pack animal had to be unloaded every night before it was turned out to graze.

In 1833 a pack train set out from St Louis. It consisted of one hundred and twenty horses with forty men in charge of them; the objectives were to buy furs from the trappers' annual meet at Wyoming, and also to set up a new trading post at the mouth of the Yellowstone river. In addition to the horses, the train consisted of a number of sheep which were to provide food for the men until they reached buffalo country, and two bulls and three cows which were to be used as breeding stock at the new post. But as the century advanced, horses, prone to disease and not sufficiently hardy for the taxing conditions of the road, were gradually replaced by the sturdier mule which, with an average working life of eighteen years, outlasted the horse.

Although the supply of mules increased rapidly, it never really met the demand. The price rose steeply in the last two decades of the great age of freighting, from about $100 each in 1850 to as much as $500 in 1870. Mules were also regularly used as draught animals and here again they involved the operator in a high capital outlay since, as compared with the ox, they demanded an elaborate and costly harness. At about $100 per wagon, it cost as much as the vehicle itself. So a twenty-team wagon train, with ten mules to the wagon, represented an investment of $25,000—and to this, of course, the operator had to add a heavy wage bill. Thus, with the dangers of loss on the road, from storms, flooded rivers or hostile Indians, the entrepreneur who went into the freighting business certainly took risks that justified the immense profits that could be made from a successful trip.

Because of the costs involved and the long period, never less than six months, during which his capital was tied up before showing any return, the operator did everything possible to cut out delays. An obvious point of economy was the time spent on the breaking of new mules and the training of teams. Instead of the days really needed for this, the wagon-master and his teamsters had only a few hours to get the mules accustomed to bit and harness, or the oxen under the yoke, and in the first week or so while the animals were learning to work together as a team the train would be lucky to cover more than three or four miles a day.

There are graphic accounts of the preparation of a team for the road. The day started at the corral where the new beasts were held for selection. First, the bullwhackers and mule drivers took stock of the situation, attempting to size up the strength and character of individual animals in the milling herd. The composition of the team was in itself a matter of some skill, since animals with quite different temperaments were required in different positions. The 'wheelers', which held the shaft of the wagon, had to be sturdy and phlegmatic beasts willing to follow the long team ahead of them, and able to hold up the weight of the wagon when it was descending steep or awkward slopes (the primitive brakes were of little help if the wheelers could not take the weight). At the head of the team came the 'leaders'; here weight was less important than intelligence and a quick response to the rein or whip in turning.

When the animals had been selected, they had to be sorted out from the rest, and the teamster could certainly expect no co-operation. He needed all his wits to avoid being crushed to death under the trampling hoofs. Once the animal was out of the mêlée it had to yoked up, and then was left to buck and protest until it was calm enough to be yoked up with a broken animal.

At any point in the long trek the men in charge had to be prepared for a stampede of mules or oxen at the slightest provocation; a whiplash landing unexpectedly at the feet of the leaders, writhing like a snake in front of them, or the flapping of a coat, might be sufficient to set them off. Then the only thing for it was to wait until they had run themselves to a standstill and pick up the pieces. A stampede on any scale might lose a day's journey time and, if the wagons were damaged, a good deal more.

Once on the road, there were many other troubles. Immediately outside the town the road was confined between the fencing put up by the local population to delimit their holdings in the prairie. The trains, which on the open plains could spread out over half a mile to avoid the muddy and broken parts of the trail, were forced to follow the wet bottoms of the rivers or climb steep bluffs. In pioneer America, as in most other parts of the contemporary world, the provision of good access roads came low on the list of community priorities. Again, the trains often had to set out very early in the year to reach the plains when the prairie grass was at its richest, so as to have fodder for the animals. This inevitably meant hitting the trail before the rains of winter were fully past and before the ground was dried out. Mud was a constant hazard. One partner in a freighting company rode out to see how his men were doing on the road, and came across a wagon up to its axles in mud; on sympathising with the driver, he was met with the reply, 'Well! I guess it's not so bad as it might be—there are two other wagons under me and they're having one hell of a time.' Life on the freight trails would often have been unbearable without a fairly sturdy sense of humour as well as a strong right arm.

The men who drove their teams over hundreds of miles of unmade and unprotected trails had to be tough. In charge of the train, the wagon-master held a position analogous to a ship's captain on the high seas, and at least one claimed that this position should be given the force of legal sanction. During the long miles between its 'port' of departure and its destination, the train was without any constituted authority, and the discipline of the forty to fifty men of various nationalities rested on the pressure of shared danger, and the strength of character and quickness of draw of the wagonmaster. However, the men who took the job were well acquainted with the hazards. On the trail any wagonmaster worth his salt enforced his word as absolute law, and mutiny was dealt with summarily. Many fully earned their reputations as tyrants; others relied on a mixture of profanity, good humour and a sure judgement of what could be done.

The vast majority were drawn from the ranks, so to speak, having served their time as teamsters. The job demanded determination, leadership and also shrewdness—one master delayed the passage of a steep descent until nightfall so that his men should not have a chance to see the steepness of the precipice they were expected to negotiate. The job also carried the responsibility for goods and equipment that might total $250,000 in value.

Pilfering was common. Any master with a freight of whisky in his load needed every day's experience of his own past to cope with techniques at a teamster's disposal for the drawing of a quick nip; and it was the man in charge who paid. One master had his pay docked $50 when the cargo arrived short of two bags of sugar sold *en route* by an enterprising bull-whacker. But the pay was good, four times that of the teamsters.

Beneath the wagonmaster there was a hierarchy headed by the mule-skinner. Riding on the nearside 'wheeler' and wielding a six-to-eight-foot whip, he might control a team of as many as sixteen mules, harnessed in eight pairs, with a single rein running from the bit of the near-side leader. Next down the scale came the bullwhacker who worked from the ground with a whip that might be anything up to twenty feet in length, directing the team of oxen with the bite and crack of the lash. Such men were rough, tough and often violent, and controlling rivalries between his team was one of the responsibilities of the master. Once the train reached its destination there was no attempt at restraint. Many masters would make an ostentatious display of generosity to their men on the first night in and then there was nothing to be done but to wait until they had spent their wages on the wine, women and luxuries of the town.

Such were the men who travelled the roads of the prairie. To some the freight was fair game for easy and illicit profit; by many masters it was viewed almost as a sacred trust. For the promoters it was a source of immense potential wealth, and for the towns of the Missouri valley, the ports of the prairie from which the trains set out, it was the foundation of their prosperity and the source of a way of life.

All winter the teamsters were lodged in town, bringing money and dis-order to the saloons and commercial quarter. In late February or early March some were on the prairie rounding up the oxen that had been sent out to winter there; others would be breaking in mules and making up teams so that before the month was out the first trains would be heading westward. From April to December there would be the constant coming and going of trains, the bringing and dispatch of merchandise and the bustle on the wharves as steamers from further east discharged their goods. Towns such as Kansas, Leavenworth, Nebraska City and even St Louis virtually lived on the wagon trade. Money came into the town not only from the profits of the merchants but also from the ancillary indus-tries and employments. Warehouses had to be built and run, mules and oxen housed and maintained and wagons serviced; above all, of course, the wagonmakers did a thriving trade. There were thirty-two wagon-wrights in St Louis in the mid-century, while in 1865 citizens of Atchison contracted to supply two thousand wagons (each of which would cost at least $100) from the town's factories.

At the far end of the long trail the pioneer communities, rich in agricul-tural produce and mining, paid handsomely for the manufactured goods brought at such labour and hazard across more than 1,000 miles of dangerous and often hostile territory. For most of the nineteenth century, the west of the United States was virtually without metalled roads, yet against all the odds the development of the continent progressed so that by the 1860s shareholders could see the value of a Union Pacific Railroad.

9

Roads in Europe and Asia in the Twentieth Century

THE MODERN MOTOR road was born in Europe and its principles developed by the militaristic regimes of pre-war Italy and Germany. In both cases social policy combined with military requirements to direct funds into road-building; only since the war have the commercial value and general social desirability of good roads been the cause of major investment. In China and Russia apparently, road-building is still largely a matter of military and political, one might almost say propaganda, priorities, but elsewhere, in the leading industrial countries, roads have displaced the railways as the main arteries of international trade and travel. Since the 1950s there have been, on paper at least, plans for a European network of 'E' roads, built to standard specifications and serving the main international trunk routes, but as with so many grand international projects the ideal is honoured more in the breach than the observance. Nevertheless, the plan for the 'E' routes is the natural goal towards which all the various national programmes should tend.

In this chapter we shall look at the history of road-building in Italy and Germany, Europe's leaders in this field; some of the major achievements in Europe as a whole; and the development of roads in Asia, with particular attention to Japan.

From fascism to tourism

By the mid-1960s the six countries of the European Economic Community, together with Britain, Austria and Switzerland, had some 4,000 miles of motor roads and of these half were in Germany and a quarter in Italy. The story began in 1922 with the accession of Benito Mussolini to power. Conventionally, his dictatorship is dated from the romantically named 'March on Rome'. (An auspicious title indeed for a regime which did so much for road-building, but unfortunately misleading since the dictator's journey from Milan to the capital was in fact made by train!) Mussolini's declared intent was to restore to Italy the glories of the Roman empire and this, it must at once be said, was not fulfilled in every particular. However, in at least two matters this pseudo-historical bombast produced lasting results. Thanks to huge investment and the advanced technology of the twentieth century, the administration was able to complete the draining of the malarial swamps known as the Pontine Marshes, which had defeated the efforts of Rome's rulers—popes and emperors—since the time of Trajan in the second century. The desire to return to Rome's past greatness produced one other practical benefit when the first *autostrada* was opened in 1924. By the end of the decade Italy could boast 320 miles of such highways. They did not reach the high standards of later work, but could reasonably be claimed as the world's first roads designed exclusively for motor traffic, since they did incorporate the two basic principles of limited access and the elimination of grade crossings. These early *autostrade* were run by private corporations and financed by tolls and advertising; they are the direct ancestors of Italy's modern trunk-road system and the forerunners of Germany's *Autobahnen*.

The economic advantages of a good road system are particularly obvious in Italy, where the highest single source of foreign currency is tourism. Consequently, road-building has enjoyed a high government priority since the war and achieved its most magnificent creation with the famous Autostrada del Sole, completed in 1964 (*see* Plate 22). It runs for almost 500 miles from Milan to Naples, linking many towns along the route, most important among them the port of Genoa and Rome itself. Travelling through some of the most beautiful and varied landscape in Europe, it necessitated the building of one hundred and thirteen major bridges, over eleven miles of tunnels and nearly six hundred flyovers. Like the first *autostrade* it is administered by a special consortium and is to be paid for out of tolls.

The German road-building programme, which has now far outstripped that of Italy, as of every other European country, was first formulated in 1930, but not properly inaugurated until 1934, the year after Hitler came to power. The first objective was no doubt military, but the political desirability of providing work for Germany's many unemployed and the general economic advantages to the country were not ignored.

The need for channelling various types of motor traffic on to special roads was foreseen as early as the year 1910 by Sidney Webb in his book *The King's Highway*, but in the first country to launch a major motor-road programme the need for careful landscaping was also appreciated from the outset (*see* Plate 16). In 1933 Dr Fritz Todt was appointed general inspector of German roads. He had previously been manager of the road-building department of the Munich construction company Sager and Woerner, and some of the success of the pre-war German road programme may be attributable to the decision to co-opt an industrial manager from industry rather than to recruit from the civil service.

Fritz Todt, confronted with the commission to build 2,500 miles of roads for the *Reichsautobahn* programme, set about his work with a thorough attention to detail. It has been claimed that he intended this military communications system to be built as a series of landscaped parkways. He engaged Professor Alwin Seifert as landscape consultant, and he and his assistants were involved in the earliest planning stages. A sketch of the planting for each section was given to the engineers before excavation; attention could thus be given to the handling of topsoil and its dumping, so as to save on subsequent earth shifting. In fact, when the design for each section was submitted for approval to the general inspector, it had to be accompanied by the comments of the landscapist. Indeed, he was referred to as the *Landschaftsanwalt*—a telling metaphor since the word literally means 'council for the defence' of the landscape against the engineer.

More advanced than their Italian forerunners, the German *Autobahnen* have been described as the world's first true expressways. By 1942 the network already extended to 1,310 miles, but because of the war, work was largely at a standstill. In 1953 the report of a government-appointed commission revealed that some 40 per cent of Germany's roads were in need of urgent repair. The result was that two years later a ten-year improvement programme was launched, and a total expenditure of £3,000 million was planned for; work has pressed on during the 1960s so that Germany has the finest network of arterial roads anywhere in the world outside the United States.

Civil engineering in the service of the road

As the pace of European road-building quickens, so the number of major engineering works grows. Achievements that would once have been the object of general admiration are now so numerous and, apparently, so technically undemanding that they are regarded as commonplace. The appearances are deceptive, however, and we shall now take a brief look at some of the more impressive undertakings that have contributed to the improvement of road travel on the Continent.

Tourism, as has been observed, is one of the major factors behind the increase in road traffic, and an important spur to the improvement of overland communications. The car is now the dominant means of passenger transport, while road haulage has more than quadrupled during the last two decades. The point is well illustrated by the case of the Netherlands, where the tonnage of freight passing the frontiers by road is equal to that of the railways. During the 1970s the trend must continue; the share of the railways will progressively decline, at least for a time, until the congestion on the roads, and the damage to living conditions and environment caused by increasingly massive vehicles, compels governments to introduce regulations forcing hauliers to use the railways.

In the Netherlands, the only country other than Italy and Germany with a motorway programme before 1939, the large river basins and the need to provide rapid transit across them have produced two important tunnels during the late 1960s. The one under the Ij estuary at Amsterdam carries four lanes of traffic over a distance somewhat less than half the length of the Mersey road tunnel, but through the most treacherous geological formation. The tunnel consists of a number of massive prefabricated reinforced concrete sections, between 230 and 295 feet in length, clad in a water-proofing of steel on the bottom and sides and of bituminous tar on the top. Because of the unstable stratum beneath the river bed, the tunnel rests on a foundation consisting of a concrete platform that stretches the whole length of the tunnel and is supported on massive piles, driven to depths as great as 260 feet to reach a firm stratum. Both slight subsidence and expansion due to temperature changes have been allowed for, the sections being jointed with steel 'bellows' and being free to shift longitudinally on the foundation by the use of special low-friction bearings. The same detailing has gone into the demands of the roadway which has an aluminium grid 'ceiling light' stretching out above the approaches to provide a steady and graduated transition from the daylight to the artificial lighting inside the tunnel.

The road crossing of the Vieille Meuse branch of the Rhine delta, south of the great port of Rotterdam, is also by tunnel. Here, at Heinenoord, it is again constructed from prefabricated sections; it has a length of 656 yards, though with approach ramps the total length is almost double that. Because of anticipated future requirements of the shipping lane, the tube of the tunnel is being sunk to a sufficient depth to allow a channel 40 feet deep and 360 feet wide. Such great feats of engineering are overshadowed by the transformation of some of the Alpine routes by the new tunnels that are being built there; yet in such mountainous terrain the road-builder has problems to face above the surface.

In the spring of 1969 an ambitious project for roofing over stretches of the Axenstrasse along Lake Lucerne was completed. Until the work was done the road had to be closed from time to time because of the danger from landslips, and to clear the debris left behind by them. But the road nevertheless continued to claim a number of victims. Even though the worst trouble occurred at known seasons, often rocks dislodged during this period were halted in their fall by a tree or some other natural obstacle and only gradually worked loose, to come crashing down on to the road unexpectedly and sometimes fatally. The new roofing extends over a total length of 4,228 feet in four sections and is supported by slabs of reinforced concrete which are supported on cantilevered sections anchored into the rockface. The roofing slabs are each 16 feet wide and 8 inches thick, being covered with a 4-inch layer of bitumen, burnt on, to act as a shock absorber. The structure is designed to withstand the impact of rocks of up to 100 pounds falling from a height of 160 feet, while boulders with as much as twice this impact would cause only superficial damage.

The engineering demands above ground may well be more taxing when the designer has to provide rapid expressways and uninterrupted interchanges in the great urban areas of the modern age. Among the most elaborate enterprises of this kind in Europe, perhaps, is the Porte de la Chapelle interchange to the north of Paris, which took three and a half years to complete.

The designers had to provide access and connections in four main directions. The interchange had first to link the main N1 national route to the north with the Paris ring road; to link this same road with the main Paris urban network; to link this network with two secondary roads serving the northern suburbs of the city; and finally to provide access to the railheads in the district. The designers' job was further complicated by the fact that the only acceptable site was already occupied by a large sports complex, comprising two football fields and a stadium; moreover, the roads had to straddle an extensive rail-marshalling yard. Such problems at ground level were solved directly and boldly by rebuilding the whole of the sporting complex at another site near by, and by carrying the road over extended flyovers on which, at some points, three traffic streams crossed one above the other.

The difficulties below ground level were if anything even greater. Two forty-inch gas mains had to be relocated without the interruption of supplies, and it was found on inspection that the main sewer, which had been intended as part of the foundations for a flyover, would not be able to withstand the pressures involved—it had to be covered with a concrete 'roof'. The whole project required the installation of a new drainage system with a total length of one mile and a quarter. The work at the Porte de la Chapelle was remarkable in its extent, but was certainly not unique. The problems that face the designer in carrying the growing densities of high-speed traffic through our ancient cities are comparable to those that confronted the builders of the great underground systems of an earlier generation.

Nor can the designers have any confidence that their solutions will be permanent, or even outlast their own lifetime. Much of Germany's current expenditure on road-building is devoted to renovating and up-dating the autobans. In 1968 the reconstruction of the Bonn–Cologne route was completed; it had involved converting the former four-lane highway, without a central reservation, into an up-to-date six-lane route, and the job had to be done without interrupting the use of the road.

By and large, the road-builder is resigned to the prospect that the traffic of tomorrow will sooner or later overtax even the best-laid plans of today, but it is questionable whether many have to contend with the dangers that confronted the municipal authorities of Omsk, in Siberia, on the occasion of the fiftieth anniversary of the Russian Revolution in 1967. In anticipation of excessive overloading from traffic and crowds of spectators, the recently built arch bridge was tested before the event by convoys of heavily laden trucks jolting across it in a series of stop starts.

The European network

In 1936 the International Association of Automobile Clubs published a map showing the existing roads it recommended for the main international highways in a European system. It also proposed the specifications that should be generally accepted for the building of these Euro-routes: minimum road widths of twenty-six feet; the elimination of all level-crossings, whether of rail or road; the installation of first-aid posts and telephones; and ancillary services, such as a standard system of inter-national road signs, adequate garaging and hotel facilities along the route. A year earlier the desirability of a London to Istanbul motorway had been mooted. By 1939 none of these proposals had advanced any nearer towards reality and the war and the turmoil that it left in its wake prevented any further work.

Consequently when, in 1950, the representatives of the nations of Europe meeting at Geneva agreed on the principle of an international network, everything was still to do. However, one essential proposal was made; it related to the basic matter of financing the new work, though it turned out not to be fully practicable. The original signatories were Austria, Belgium, Bulgaria, the Federal German Republic, France, Great Britain, Greece, Holland, Italy, Luxembourg, Norway, Poland,

16 The German *Autobahnen* of the 1930s incorporated almost all the principles of the modern motor road. Notice the central strip, the use of existing woodlands to help landscape the road, and the careful merging of the feeder and exit routes into the main carriageways. The great drawback of these pioneer roads was their undeviating straightness, which easily caused driver-fatigue and boredom.

17 Technically Italy's roads during the inter-war years were second to none, but the free use of advertising detracted from the beauties of the landscape. Elsewhere too, and notably in the United States, billboards rapidly sprang up along new roads.

18 Continuous surface-spreading is now a commonplace, but it was far from familiar when this machine was at work on the German autobahns in the 1930s.

19 The Grossglocknerstrasse, one of the major Alpine roads, during construction in 1963. In many places it was necessary to build out from the mountainside to accommodate the wide roadway.

20 The seven-mile tunnel through Mont Blanc, under construction in 1959.

21
The Chinese military road from Shanghai to Tibet, built in 1955.

22 Tunnels and viaducts of the famous Italian Autostrada del Sole, on the stretch between Bologna and Florence.

23 A view of a toll-gate on the No. 3 Kei-Hin highway joining Yokohama and the outskirts of Tokyo. This is a six-lane, limited-access expressway.

24 An interchange on the Meishin Expressway at Otsu. This 120-mile toll road connects four of Japan's largest cities, Kobe, Osaka, Kyoto and Nagoya.

25 A vivid example of the way in which the construction of new motorways in big cities like London devastates former residential districts. In this case protests by local resident associations made the road-builders change the route so as to by-pass certain houses.

26
Progress is not ideal for everybody; this picture was taken under Britain's M1 and such disasters in planning are all too common in modern road building.

27 The Hollywood Freeway, Los Angeles.

28 A fly-over under construction on the M4 outside Bristol.

29 Such mini electric 'transporters' may be obligatory in the cities of the future; they have already been introduced in Santa Barbara, California, to reduce traffic congestion.

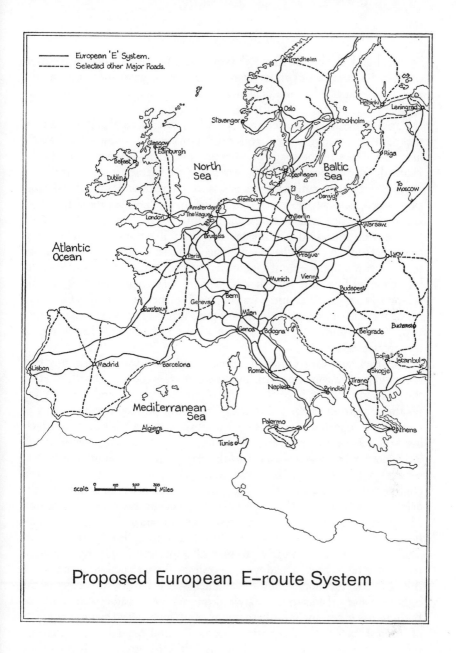

European 'E' System.
Selected other Major Roads.

Trondheim

Helsinki
Leningrad

Oslo
Stavanger
Stockholm

Riga

Glasgow
Edinburgh
Belfast
North
Sea
Baltic
Sea
Dublin
Copenhagen
To
Moscow

Hamburg
Danzig

Amsterdam
The Hague
London
Berlin
Warsaw

Atlantic
Ocean
Brussels

Paris
Prague
Lvov

Munich
Vienna
Budapest

Geneva
Bern
Bucharest
Bordeaux
Milan
Genoa
Bologna
Belgrade

Madrid
Barcelona
Sofia
To
Istanbul
Lisbon
Rome
Skopje

Naples
Brindisi
Tirane

Mediterranean
Sea
Palermo
Algiers

Athens
Tunis

scale 0 100 200 300
Miles

Proposed European E-route System

Portugal and Spain, Sweden, Turkey and Yugoslavia. The declaration
envisaged a network of more than 37,000 miles, gave specifications for
design and expected traffic densities and even attended to such important
ancillary matters as the regulation of advertising.

Various revisions followed in 1957, when further emphasis was laid on
the matter of interchanges, and regulations were outlined that would
limit the access to the roads of adjoining properties. However, up to the
1960s the declaration remained very much a declaration. Apart from the
obvious fact that national interests were overriding international considerations, this may be in part explained by the total failure of the over-
ambitious finance scheme to get off the ground. Monsieur P. Le Vert of
France, who addressed the International Road Federation on the progress
of the network at its Madrid Conference in 1962, summed up the reasons
for this with a fine blend of Gallic elegance and irony. The failure of the
international financing system was, he said, due to an extremely simple
reason—'*a priori*, no country was opposed to the creation of a European
fund, but each understood itself to figure in it as receiving a sum larger
than its contribution; yet the simple addition of demands has never, so
far, created resources'.

Six years later an editorial in *World Road News* was complaining that
the nations of Europe were still almost exclusively concerned with meeting
the transport demands of their own highway systems, and were paying
no attention to international routes. The writer pointed out that many of
Germany's superb highroads stop dead at the country's borders. The feel-
ing was echoed by implication in a speech by the German Minister of
Transport, who looked forward to the day when his country's excellent
network might form the hub of a European system. As it is, the grand
continental network is little more than a series of route numbers over
existing roads, rather than specially designed or reconstructed routes.
Many great works have been undertaken and others are in active preparation, such as the bridge over the Bosphorus from European to Asian
Turkey, but there is no early prospect of a concerted effort by the countries involved to press ahead with co-ordinated construction. Irritating as
this is to the 'technocrat' and the engineers, it is hardly surprising in the
light of history. Indeed, if a standard international road system could be
built across a continent with so many, and such deep, historic conflicts
of interest, before the formation of some form of federal administration,
the event would be unique in history. Hitherto, great roadworks have
been the result of a powerful central authority overriding local interests,
and despite the great hopes of a few years ago, Europe shows no signs of
establishing such an authority.

The roads of Japan

Japan began to make serious provision for a modern road-building programme in the early 1950s; in June 1965 the first Japanese freeway was opened to the public. Since that date many other routes have come into service and the rate of progress over the next fifteen years will be dramatic. This first freeway is about 120 miles long, and connects the two important industrial areas of Osaka/Kobe with Nagoya in the Chubu district of central Japan. The road is known as the Meishin Expressway; it consists of a four-lane highway, each carriageway being about twelve feet wide, and has a central reservation planted with bushes to cut the glare of oncoming headlights (*see* Plate 24). There are only 14 access points along the whole distance (as opposed to 20 on an equivalent stretch of the English M1) but there are, perhaps surprisingly, 31 bus stops as well as 7 parking areas and 4 service areas. It was planned as the southern part of the Tokyo–Kobe motorway first mooted during the war, when a preliminary survey was conducted.

Five years after the opening of the road from Kobe to Nagoya, the whole route to Tokyo was made available to high-speed traffic with the building of the Tomei Expressway between Tokyo and Nagoya, a distance of 220 miles. At its completion it was regarded as the highpoint of Japanese transportation engineering. Many lessons had been learnt during the building of the southern stretch, and since the road runs through rough terrain it demanded outstanding technical expertise to bring it to a successful completion after seven years' work. A particularly remarkable achievement is the Sakawagawa bridge, a handsome curving viaduct, that carries the road at the height of some 200 feet across a beautiful river valley which is dominated by the splendour of Mount Fuji in the distance. The curve, with other features of the design, helps to lessen the impact of the road on the landscape, and the same device is used on the bridge spanning the narrows where the road crosses Lake Hamana.

Japanese engineers work in one of the most beautiful landscapes in the world, and come from a tradition in which the love of landscape has been, for centuries, at the centre of aesthetic experience. Despite the pressing demand for transport facilities, and the astonishing programmes to which they are working, Japan's road-builders have continued in this tradition and have displayed to the full that typically Japanese talent for the natural blending of the twentieth century with the beauties of the past.

Some of the finest examples of highway landscaping in Japan are to be found on the Nittsu Fujimi Parkway in the mountains of the Izu peninsula and on the Fujimiya toll road, which takes full advantage of its magnificent site below the slopes of Mount Fuji. The cascade of hairpin bends negotiated by the Irohazaka toll road in the Nikko National Park, as the road snakes its way out of the steep and tree-covered valleys, rivals some astonishing climbs in the Alps; the route, renamed the Izu Skyline Road, emerges to traverse the crest of the mountains like some modern ridgeway. However, elsewhere the road, instead of blending with its background or pointing up the features of the landscape, is a brash and uncompromising symbol of the twentieth century. One thinks particularly of the toll-gates on the Chuo Expressway, a branch of the Tomei Expressway through Fuji-yoshida, where the road broadens out to almost four times its normal width and becomes a clutter of queueing or parked vehicles awaiting their turn to pass the check points.

Ambitious targets for road improvement will mean further great disturbances to the landscape. On 31 May 1969 the Japanese government approved a national plan for development during the following fifteen years affecting every aspect of Japanese life and revolutionising the road network. It was estimated that between 1965 and 1985 land used for roads and residential purposes will have more than doubled, and this in a country where 48 per cent of the population was already crammed into the great urban centres occupying 1·2 per cent of the land area. The backbone of the transport system will be along the sinuous line from Sapporo, in the island of Hokkaido, in the north, through Sendai, Tokyo, Nagoya, Osaka, Hiroshima and Fukuoka, in the island of Kyushu in the south. An important part will be played by the high-speed railways, such as that already operating along the famous Tokaido strip, but the place of the roads will become central. The two lengths of expressway that we have mentioned here will become part of a massive 1,000-mile system linking these seven large industrial areas, and sending out branches to many smaller towns along the route. In total, it is planned to build 3,500 miles of trunk highways before 1985, while air terminals and ports will also be expanded and developed.

The statistics of traffic trends, as well as the overall growth of the Japanese economy, reveal some of the reasons for these far-reaching proposals. According to a government white paper for the financial year ending April 1968, the overall transport activity had more than doubled since the beginning of the decade, while road transport increased 25 per cent over the previous year. More interesting, since it shows Japan conforming to the general pattern for advanced industrial nations, was the fact that while the bulk of freight traffic was carried by coastal shipping, to be expected in a country made up of a number of islands, road transport came second and the railways third. In passenger traffic the figures are somewhat different, but though the trend revealed has been slower in gathering momentum, it is clearly the same. Overall, the railways, which it should be remembered still carry the bulk of commuter traffic, had a 61 per cent share of the total, while 37 per cent is accounted for by private cars, the remaining small fraction being shared between shipping and airlines. Against these figures we must set the fact that car ownership increased by a remarkable 41 per cent over the previous year and the trend is continuing. The relevance of these facts to the trunk road is obvious, but so also is their significance in terms of urban congestion.

One-third of Japan's total population is concentrated in the two industrial and residential centres of Tokyo, reckoned the world's largest city, and Osaka, and these two regions together account for more than half of the total transport demands of the country. The increase in car ownership has now reached such a level that the expansion of road development in Tokyo is approaching its limit. Faced with this situation, the Japanese, with hard-headed realism, have officially recognised what has been apparent in all the great cities of the world for some time now, that what is needed is a reorganisation of the functions of the city, and the distribution of its various activities over a wider area of the main conurbation. It is proposed that such activities as administration, industry and education be distributed among well-defined districts on the urban periphery, and that a network of high-speed rail and road links between these regions should be built to anticipate this shift of activity. Finally a system of road-pricing is being considered, whereby the users of the new transport facilities should be expected to finance them as directly as possible.

In constructing expressways in existing urban areas the full range of solutions open to the modern engineer is being deployed by Japanese designers in an attempt to reduce the impact of these thoroughfares on the city areas through which they pass. The main region for development is the Osaka/Kobe complex, and it is planned to link the heart of the two districts by motorway. In addition to the familiar elevated roadway, tunnels and sunken channels will also be used to carry the road. It is estimated that the total length of urban motorways in the region will be between sixty and seventy miles by the end of 1971. The central part of the development is already open to traffic, and the building programme was planned so as to accommodate the increased traffic generated by the World Exposition held in 1970.

Because of her very high population density and the comparatively low proportion of her land surface open to development, Japan is confronted with all the problems of congestion common to the world situation in the second half of the twentieth century, but in a peculiarly aggravated form. As should be clear from the outline given here, however, transport rightly enjoys a high priority, and the Japanese road system is one of the most sophisticated in the world.

Some roads in Asia

Perhaps the most celebrated highway of recent Asian history is the
notorious military road built by the Chinese authorities from the western
region of the Chinese province of Sinkiang to the autonomous region of
Tibet (*see* Plate 21). Its route lay through the virtually uninhabited and
mountainous region of Ladakh, and its building was one of the prime
causes of a boundary dispute between China and India that in the early
1960s seemed at times to threaten the world with war. The rights and
wrongs of the dispute can hardly be entered into here, but the episode is
of considerable interest as a case study of the importance of roads as a
political fact.

In the nineteenth century China, weakened internally and slow to
come to terms with the industrial process so rapidly adopted by her
neighbour Japan, was the prey of the more advanced nations of the west.
From Russia to Great Britain the historic states of Europe plundered the
ancient civilisation of wealth and territory, and established claims and
boundaries that could not be contested until China had begun to recover
something of her ancient strength and confidence under the communist
regime of Mao Tse-tung.

Among the territories that had been able to throw off their age-old
allegiance to the ancient Chinese empire was Tibet. In the early 1950s
Communist armies reconquered the country, however, and from that
time onwards there were numerous reports of road-building from
Tibet to the neighbouring Chinese provinces. In 1955 China and India
signed an agreement over the problem of Tibet, and in December two
roads were inaugurated leading out of Lhasa. One travelled north-east a
distance of 1,400 miles, to Sining in Tsinghai province, at an average
height of 9,800 feet above sea level; the other, 1,300 miles long, ran in
a more northerly direction to Paan in the province of Sikang, at an
average height of 12,000 feet.

Two years later the 700-mile-long motor road from south-west Sinkiang
to Tibet was begun, and in the same year the Chinese authorities let it
be known that there was a total of 3,000 miles of roads available to motor
traffic in Tibet. It was clear from her road-building that China was
determined to make good her newly regained province, and in the ensuing
years tension between her and India mounted over the frontier region.
In 1959 China was engaged on building programmes in the north-
western and south-western provinces, so as to open them to motor traffic,
where formerly only pack-animals could travel. She was also building
feeder roads from the Lhasa–Sinkiang highway. In the same year India
began her preparations by building roads to her frontier with Chinese
Tibet.

Russia, the other great Asian power, has published little information on her road programme, but in 1956 she embarked on a major project for an expressway leading out of Moscow to improve rapid east/west communications, and to facilitate the evacuation of the capital in time of war. In 1959 a road designed, it was said, for tourist traffic was opened from the Finnish frontier to Moscow via Leningrad. But as a matter of general policy Russia has relied on rail and air links for long-distance travel over her vast territories; private cars are still few, and the poor state of Russia's roads is not crucial to the country's transport system. Yet, as the newly discovered mineral resources of Siberia are opened up, and new towns and industrial centres are built, roads will follow. The motor-car, the symbol of the second stage of the industrial revolution, can be expected to force massive investment in road-building in Russia as she advances into the club of the rich consumer societies.

IO

The Roads of America in the Twentieth Century

IN TRANSPORT AS in every other aspect of material civilisation, the United States of America offers to the world the model of its future. In this chapter we shall be studying many beautiful roads which reveal the engineer's art in its finest aspects and demonstrate the extent to which the rich societies of the twentieth century depend on goods and amenities, formerly regarded as the luxuries of the city-dweller, being transported to the most remote communities. We shall also get a glimpse of the way in which living patterns and even modes of thought have become inextricably bound up with the concrete of the highways. For it was in America that the motor-car began its transformation of western society, and it is there that it is still at work, producing what may be classed as the greatest single revolution in Man's way of life since the discovery of the art of agriculture.

Roads and a changing society

From that remote period in the neolithic age when men first began to till the soil and produce for themselves the means of life, all the higher achievements of material civilisation have been the products of sedentary cultures. Their foci are in great cities and their means of support derive from the rural hinterland and the processes of trade. But in the future, with the population explosion and with freedom of movement possible for almost every citizen, the idea of 'centres' of civilisation will be outmoded; mobility will be the natural condition of life.

The nature of the automobile revolution is observable around us and its potential consequences are well known—nevertheless the figures are breathtaking. Between 1910 and 1916 the American car 'population' increased fivefold to a total of 2·3 million. In the next half century the increase was by a factor of almost forty: by 1964 there was the astonishing total of 86 million cars on America's roads. By the end of this century this is expected to increase to 316 million private vehicles, enough for every American man, woman and child. In Aldous Huxley's *Brave New World* the new era was dated from the advent of Our Ford, and whatever else the future may hold we can be sure that if *Homo Sapiens*, as he is sometimes laughingly called, survives to the year 2000, then the more materially advanced of his species will still be travelling by some form of 'personalised' transport, the direct descendant of the first empire of Detroit.

The road is no longer simply a route from here to there, a transportation link between two distinct communities; it is a part of the landscape and, since more and more people spend an appreciable amount of their life at the wheel, either on the way to work or touring on holiday, a part of our very experience of life. It is one of the major factors in the destruction of the cities, and it is giving rise to a new kind of megalopolis more fitted to the conditions of the overpopulated world of tomorrow.

Los Angeles is the classic 'city of the future'. It has been estimated that of the total area covered by this vast conurbation, one-third is taken up by road surface, one-third by parking facilities and one-third by 'living space'. As more people become richer they demand, while it can be had, more spacious accommodation; since each has at his or her disposal the means of personal long-distance travel, space must be found to accommodate the vehicles in movement and at rest. The idea of the neighbourhood becomes displaced by overlapping networks of friendship; people can choose their neighbours over a 100-mile radius and the 'city' becomes a conglomerate of separate households linked by a mesh of motorways.

Second only to the investment in weapons of war and systems of defence, the automobile industry in the United States is the biggest single consumer of capital and manpower. Indeed, in all major industrial countries the vigour of the motor industry is one of the surest measures of the overall health of the economy.

Until the launching of the Interstate Highway System in 1956, scheduled for completion in 1972, road design and building in the United States had been primarily confined to the improvement, often considerable, of a network already in existence. Between 1921 and 1960, the total estimated mileage of roads and streets rose from 2,925,000 to 3,546,000, an increase of 21 per cent (in this period the population rose by 70 per cent and the number of car registrations went up sevenfold). But while part of this increase represented the opening up of entirely new routes, some to give access to new areas for recreational purposes and others to serve the war effort, by far the greater part was accounted for by the new urban streets. But if few new routes were opened up the conditions of travel were greatly changed for the better: whereas in 1921 only 387,000 miles of road were paved, by 1960 there were 2,557,000 miles; similarly, 1960's figure of 34,190 miles of multi-lane carriageway represented a vast improvement on the situation forty years previously when few roads were more than double-lane.

The road-planner and -builder struggles hard to save himself from falling too far behind the ever-advancing tide of increasing traffic. The circle is as classic as it is vicious: as the roads improve, so they are more freely used. Not only did the number of private cars multiply seven times in the forty years under consideration but the average mileage travelled by each very nearly doubled. Thus, while the inadequate U.S. network of 1921 had to cope with 55,000 million-vehicle miles per annum, the much improved but still inadequate system of 1960 was handling 738,000 million.

Most planners would probably agree that there is no guaranteed formula for forward planning in transport. There are too many unknown factors. Every important state and city is conducting traffic surveys in an endeavour to analyse current usage of the system, but whether their findings truly represent what people want as opposed to what they are forced to do is debatable. The number of journeys that are not undertaken because the limitations of the present highways make them inconvenient can hardly be estimated.

In terms of vehicle movement, the private driver is largely responsible for the increasing congestion on the roads. In 1961 it was estimated that truck movements accounted for only 18 per cent of the total, while the part played by public transport is slight and declines every year. In many smaller cities it has entirely disappeared while even in the larger centres the percentage of private travel is rarely below 85 per cent. But the trend for transport of all kinds to take to the road has been marked. In 1929, 73 per cent of all freight was carried on the railways, 23 per cent on canal and pipelines and only 4 per cent on the roads; in 1954 rail accounted for just under 51 per cent, the roads having moved up to a 16 per cent share; in 1956 freight carried by rail dropped to below 50 per cent of the total for the first time and by 1960 roads were carrying a fifth of the total.

The importance of the car manufacturers in national production has been mentioned, and the curve describing the growth of the Gross National Product, adjusted to constant dollars, and that describing the growth of vehicle miles, are hardly distinguishable until the mid-1950s. Then the growth in traffic went up slightly more sharply than the G.N.P. and it is perhaps interesting that 1957 was the first year in which more people were employed in service industries than in production.

Such a statistic is of course a measure of the extent to which the constant improvements in production techniques yield a higher standard of living. The fact that no system as yet has been devised to correct the inequalities of society (America has 5 million unemployed and an estimated 20 million living at or below the officially defined level of poverty) does not cancel the fact that in a society where more people are employed in ministering to wishes than in producing necessities, the majority are, in material terms, identifiably better off than at any other time in the world's history. And the expectations and way of life of the well-to-do majority are mirrored in the roads of America.

Perhaps the brightest achievements of her road-builders are to be found in the numerous and well-designed scenic parkways, which are as much a means of relaxation as of transport. Often planned through areas of great natural beauty, they are designed and built to enhance the amenities they serve, and in many cases are provided with by-roads and picnic areas where the holiday-maker can get as near to the untouched beauties of nature as modern man's devotion to the internal combustion engine will permit.

The first divided highways were built in the 1930s but the principle was firmly established in the philosophy of American road-designers by the report of the Highway Research Board's committee on the problems of roadside development published in 1943. The report defined the concept of the 'complete highway' and emphasised a number of points that road-designers now generally accept. The central proposition was that the utility, safety, beauty and economic functioning of the road were interdependent. The closer the design of the road to its function the more the value of the adjoining land was enhanced; good landscaping of the verges and central reservation demanded easy inclines and hence led to cheaper maintenance; a beautiful and interesting road keeps the driver alert and thus improves the safety factor. These points in general receive fuller treatment in Chapter 13, but there are a number of examples from American practice that are relevant here.

The long-distance traffic passing along the roads of the world has been a source of profit to the wayside communities since time immemorial. In twentieth-century America, shanty towns of filling stations and hot-dog stands, housing and industrial estates, sprang up overnight. Yet because the holder of property abutting the public highway is guaranteed by American common law access to that highway and, by implication, the right to park vehicles on it, such mushroom developments not only destroyed the very amenity of speed that the road had been built to provide but, as a result, undermined the source of the property-owner's prosperity since drivers tended to seek less-congested routes. It was to meet this uneconomic misuse of the highway that a new concept was developed and applied. The freeway has been described as 'a strip of land dedicated to movement, over which the abutting land has no right of light, air or access'. The contribution of the great freeways themselves to the improvement of overland communications will be described later; here it is only necessary to quote one particularly well-known example of how application of the principle of a controlled access road brings additional wealth to the community it serves. This is the case of the Boston circumferential highway or ring road, Route 128, which was the subject of careful study and analysis during the period of its building and for some time afterwards.

Designed in the first place to divert through traffic from the centre of the city to its perimeter and to afford easy communication between the suburban communities, it soon became a major arterial road in its own right and was the subject of numerous adjustments and modifications as more and more industries bought sites along the route. Despite controlled access, the advantages of establishing a factory just off the motorway, but well fed by the numerous service roads, were considerable. Such sites offered quick access to a rapid new trunk route; land values were naturally cheaper at first than in the downtown districts; more parking facilities could be provided and employees found their journeys to work greatly eased. Many managements also appreciated the strategically placed advertising that the motorway offered.

The road was opened in 1957 and two years later more than $137 million had been invested in new plant employing 27,500 workers. Some of the businesses which took premises were from out of town, others were entirely new ventures, but most of them were Boston firms which had decided to move their office locations from the centre. Altogether it has been calculated that the new road produced a net gain to the business investment represented by the metropolitan area of $129 million; more spacious premises encouraged greater production and on an average the companies increased their staff by 25 per cent. Few staff members left; few needed to move house—the improved road communications ensured accessibility; it was also observed that few of the staff lived on the residential estates bordering the highway, while the new shopping centres that sprang up drew their clientele from the metropolitan area as a whole.

The parkway concept

The Bronx River Parkway, completed in 1923, was an augury of the future. It seems probable that before the centenary of its building is celebrated the internal combustion powered vehicle that it was built to serve will be a luxury enjoyed by the few for leisure cruising. The everyday business of transport will be carried on by electric-powered passenger vehicles centrally controlled by computer and permitting the 'driver' the minimum of personal direction. The volume of traffic is likely to be so great that the pleasure drive on well-landscaped highways to rural beauty spots will be a rare and expensive one. The parkways, of which the Bronx river was the first, were originally conceived as additions to the facilities of the motor-car user—they may in the future prove to be his last refuge from the automated traffic trains that will dominate transport in all the great conurbations.

The Bronx river project was a four-lane road flanked with parkland and with access only at a limited number of points; it passed through the valley of the river and the crossroads were carried over it so that traffic intersections were eliminated. The origin of the Parkway had nothing to do with highway planning or traffic congestion but with another problem which bulks as large in the modern world—that of environmental pollution. The original sponsors of the project were the members of the New York Zoological Society, and the man who started the ball rolling was a gentleman with the remarkable name of William White Niles.

In the first year of the new century Niles and the director of the Society, a Mr Hornaday, went on a visit to Europe where Hornaday went to pay his respects to the Scottish-born American millionaire and steel king, Andrew Carnegie. While his friend went on to beard the Laird of Skibo, Niles remained at the nearby town of Inverness and spent the afternoon taking a walk on the banks of the River Ness. As he emerged from the outskirts of the town he was astonished to observe that the river appeared to be as clear downstream as it was upstream of the city. Niles admitted that he was only applying a visual test—more positive though possibly fatal results could, of course, have been obtained by drinking some of the water. Nevertheless, the contrast with the fouled waters of his native town was startling and on his return to the States the condition of the charming little Bronx river so disturbed him that he decided something must be done. His first objective was to canvass support from members of the New York Zoological Society, which owned some of the land through which the river ran. Generally the reaction was favourable, but positive assistance only came in 1904 when the director, Mr Hornaday, discovered that some of the rare water birds in the Society's care were suffering from damage and ill-health that could be clearly attributed to the filthy state of the river.

Encouraged in his campaign, Niles set about lobbying the city administration to acquire sufficient land along the length of the river on both banks to ensure that the casual pollution of its water be stopped. In 1907 he had his reward: a bill was passed which provided for the acquisition of the lands, and the whole area was laid out as a park, through which ran the motor road carrying trippers from the Botanical Gardens in Bronx Park to the Kensico Dam. The example was followed and during the 1920s and early 1930s other authorities set aside funds for similar projects. Westchester County appropriated some $80 million for parks and parkways, while New York State, acting through the Westchester County Park Commission, acquired land and rights of way to continue the original Bronx River Parkway from the Kensico Dam to the Bear Mountain Ridge, where it now connects with the southerly end of the Taconic State Parkway. This road, running through the breathtaking scenery of the state park established as a recreational area in the Taconic Mountains (where the boundaries of New York, Massachusetts and Connecticut meet), is one of the proudest achievements of American road-building.

A number of other parkways were constructed in the New York area during the 1930s, due to the efforts of the Long Island State Park Commission under its chairman Robert Moses, while the National Park Service began the Skyline Drive in the Blue Ridge mountains of Virginia. This extends from the Shenandoah National Park in Virginia to the Great Smoky National Park in North Carolina and Tennessee, a distance of some 500 miles. In 1934 the National Park Service also established the Natchez Trace Parkway which it was intended should follow the historic trail and form a permanent monument to one of the most important of America's early roads. The road is planned for a total length of 450 miles and by the mid-1960s well over half of this had been built.

Besides the continued construction of scenic parkways the post-war decades have witnessed a large expansion in the programme of major expressways. These often embody general parkway principles in so far as the value of proper landscaping is becoming increasingly recognised. The distinction between parkway and arterial expressway is becoming more artificial than real.

We have mentioned the important report of the Highway Research Committee published during the war and its influence can be seen on the number of roads built or commenced during the late 1940s. Among these were the Dallas–Fort Worth Expressway in Texas, the extension to the Henry G. Shirley Memorial Expressway; the Maine Turnpike and the first sections of the New York State Thruway, begun in 1946. Drawing their funds from tolls and federal or state funds, many more important road projects have been undertaken, but we end this brief survey with a description of the most ambitious project in road-building so far launched in America or, indeed, anywhere in the world.

Interstate highways

Though on its completion it will represent only 1 per cent of the total U.S. road mileage, the scope of the enterprise is fantastic. When the National System of Interstate and Defense Highways is complete, it will be more than six times as long as the total mileage of autobahns that the Germans hope to have in operation during the 1970s. True, the route will lie for about 30 per cent of its length over existing, federally aided primary

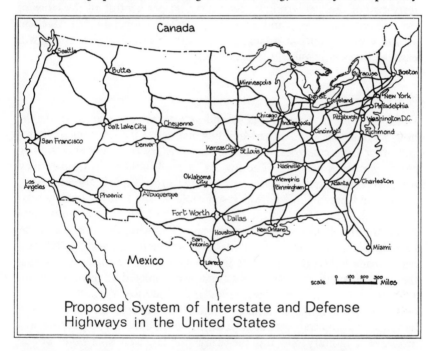

Proposed System of Interstate and Defense Highways in the United States

roads or toll roads, but it is estimated that the remainder of the net-work will be built over new rights of way. Completion is scheduled for the mid-1970s, and traffic volume forecasts up to the year 1975 have been used in drawing up the plans. Inevitably, the whole project is under criticism in some quarters for failing to plan far enough ahead, but such criticisms are the lot of all transport planners and it is perhaps difficult to visualise any time scale within the realms of practical possibility that would be viable for the longest-term needs. Roads are one of the few commodities that have not as yet adapted themselves to the demands of the 'disposable' age. They are still built to last and we may guess that the next real revolution in road-building techniques will come with the invention of an easily disposable or adaptable surface. Meanwhile planners are content to acquire more land than is needed for immediate traffic levels so that additional lanes can be built alongside the highway as the volume increases.

Although it is such a small fraction of the total U.S. road mileage the interstate system is expected to carry at least a quarter of the traffic flow. This is a sufficient measure of its importance in the peace-time economy, but both the title of the system and the Congressional Bill that brought it into being leave no doubt about the military purpose it was intended to serve. These defence highways extend for 41,000 miles in all and link forty-two of the state capitals; they serve 90 per cent of all the cities of over 50,000 inhabitants and about half the rural population of America. In the event of nuclear attack the carefully planned road network will ease, as far as is possible, the evacuation of the cities.

Roads in Canada

During the 1960s, Canada was second only to her great southern neighbour among the world's road-building nations. Like the United States and other large countries, she has a vast territory requiring an extensive communications network. The history of road-building in Canada may reasonably be dated from the work of the great French administrator, Samuel de Champlain, who was responsible for the first road in the province in the year 1606. As the colony developed, farm settlements grew up on the riverbanks, and the countryside, following the example of the French mother country, was divided up between *seigneuries*; rough and ready roads linked the farms along the river valleys and, as in Europe, the local farmers and their labourers were obliged to give a certain amount of time to the maintenance and clearance of these primitive routes. In 1721, however, a major project was undertaken. This was the building of a highway between Montreal and Quebec. The purpose was primarily a military one and the army was largely responsible for the building and upkeep of the new road. A *Grand Voyer*, after the French model, was appointed to supervise the work on this and other roadworks. But as the eighteenth century progressed, although the military continued to play an important part, the civil authorities also began to take an interest in overland transport. The pattern was little changed in its essentials when in 1760 Canada fell to the English. By the first decade of the nineteenth century all the provincial governments had road programmes in hand.

Immense territory and comparatively small population have marked the history of Canada since the earliest years and are reflected in the nature of her road-building. Labour on the roads could be raised by government order even into the nineteenth century when funds were raised for the building from taxes, and for long after this local communities were expected to maintain the roads that ran through their areas. Some roads built in this early period served existing communities and were expected to yield a financial return; these were often built and maintained by toll companies, after the English pattern, but other roads, provided by the civil and military authorities, were planned to encourage settlers to open up new territories. However, here, as elsewhere, roads came a poor second to the railways. Even when, at the time of Federation in 1867, transport came under federal administration, the railway and even inland waterways enjoyed priority; roads remained where they had always been—in the hands of provincial and local governments.

The arrival of the motor-car brought improvements, but they were slow. By 1914 matters were so bad that the Canadian Good Roads Association was founded by a group of private citizens 'to get the motor vehicle out of the mud'. It has remained one of the most important bodies in Canadian transport, though its function now is largely that of a co-ordinator of research effort. It also acts as a kind of 'parliament' for the exchange of ideas and information between members of the federal, provincial and local civil service, the road-builders, manufacturers of machinery, car-makers and trucking associations.

In the decade between 1950 and 1960 the number of vehicle miles travelled on Canadian roads more than doubled. To meet the rapidly rising demand, limited and controlled expressways were being built, as were many new high-capacity bridges. In addition, municipal and local governments initiated a number of traffic studies to provide the information essential for any realistic appraisal of future developments and transport requirements.

The Trans-Canada Highway

Although local and provincial governments have retained a central position in the Canadian road programme, the federal administration of necessity played a dominant role in the most dramatic and magnificent project so far completed. This was the Trans-Canada Highway. The idea of a coast-to-coast highway had been a dream from at least the beginning of the twentieth century, and in 1911 the Canadian Highways Association offered a medal to the first person to make the transcontinental crossing by car. Fifteen years later a photographer did in fact make the crossing. It took five and a half weeks and although the winner met the terms of the sponsors and travelled by car over the whole route, there were several tracts where the roads gave out altogether. In true pioneering spirit the 'explorer' adapted himself to the conditions that he found and fitted flanged wheels to his car so that he could avail himself of the Trans-Canadian Railway.

The full distance of the modern road, coast to coast, is 4,876 miles and the difficulties met with in its building were immense. In one stretch through the Terra Nova National Park, where the terrain is mostly rock and muskeg, the ground had to be excavated to a depth of twenty-five feet and some 175,000 cubic yards per mile had to be shifted at a cost of close on $500,000 a mile; on one seven-mile passage through the Rocky Mountains the cost exceeded $1 million a mile; while the necessity of building snow sheds to protect against the danger of avalanches in the Glacier National Park in British Columbia raised the cost to $3½ million. These sums, gigantic as they are, are most interesting for what they represent in terms of the bitter hardship and determined courage of the men who drove this mighty highway across some of the world's most inhospitable territory.

The project was initiated by the Trans-Canada Highway Act in 1949 and was opened to traffic in 1962. The cost was to be shared on a fifty-fifty basis by the federal and provincial governments, though the work in progress was to be inspected by federally appointed engineers.

The stark conditions of the arctic regions of Canada call for heroic efforts on the part of engineers and builders if anything is to be achieved at all, but the building of the Alaskan Highway almost defies the imagination. Stretching from Dawson Creek in British Columbia to the town of Fairbanks in Alaska, it has a total length of 1,523 miles and was completed in the barely credible time of six months between March and September 1942. We have seen how the demands of war have often produced some of the most important roads and this was no exception. In the last stretch on its way to Fairbanks the road was able to make use of the existing Richardson Highway, but by far the greater part was built to the design of U.S. Army engineers and by U.S. troops to supply the forces based in Alaska. For the duration of the war the whole road was under the auspices of the American military authorities, but in 1946 the Canadian section was handed over to Canadian jurisdiction and a year later the whole road was opened to general purpose traffic.

The Pan American Highway

The ideal of the 'New World' has been one of the dreams of American political thought since the nineteenth century. The founding fathers of the United States who signed the Declaration of Independence in 1783 saw their new state as the home of democratic freedom, the refuge of human dignity from the corruption and oppression of a decadent Europe. As the nineteenth century progressed, this ideal was given political body by the proclamation of the Monroe Doctrine, which stated that the United States would regard European intervention in American affairs, either North or South, as an act of war. Yet despite the ideals that it claimed to embody, the Doctrine may be regarded as merely an old-world declaration of a sphere of interest. Whatever the protestations of American politicians, the economic influence of the United States has been a predominating factor in the affairs of South America throughout this century, and the Pan American Highway system, linking the capitals of all the states of the American continent, is now at the point of becoming a reality.

In 1880, at the height of the railway fever in the north, a U.S. Congressman proposed a Pan American railroad. At that time, however, the industrialisation to the south was barely begun and only gathered speed when the railway era was giving way to that of the automobile. Apart from the rail systems of Argentina, south-west Brazil, Uruguay, Chile and Mexico, almost entirely built by British engineers and contractors, there was little basis for the construction of an all-America rail link, and by the 1920s the idea of an international highway system was being mooted. In 1925 the first Pan American road congress was held in Buenos Aires and successive congresses held to the dream of an integrated intercontinental network.

Like the planned European network of international roads, the Pan American Highway is for the greater part of its 30,000 miles a series of long-distance routes over existing roads and not a massive construction programme of a completely new highway. By 1966, for example, just over two-thirds of the total mileage was paved, 6,500 miles had a compacted all-weather surface, some 900 miles were passable in dry weather only and 800 miles were officially described as impassable to motor-traffic, a crucial stretch being the so-called Darien Gap in the Isthmus of Panama. As we shall see, plans are now afoot to close this, but at the moment the motorist travelling between the two halves of the continent is obliged to ship his car from the Venezuelan port of La Guaira to Panama.

From Panama the road leads north to the Mexican town of Nuevo Laredo, on the frontier with the state of Texas. This stretch, which has a number of alternative routes, has a total length of 3,400 miles. Thanks to the co-operation of the governments of Guatemala, El Salvador and Honduras, and heavy investment by the United States, particularly during the war years, the route offers a fine paved highway throughout. From La Guaira the highway leads along the *autopista* completed in 1950 to Caracas, the capital of Venezuela, thence on to the Colombian capital of Bogota and south-west to Quito and the coast. From here the road travels southwards, down the western coast of the continent, through Lima to Santiago and Concepción in Chile. From Santiago the road strikes across Argentina to Buenos Aires; here two main branches take the traveller to Asunción, capital of Paraguay, to the west, and to Monte-video, São Paulo and Rio de Janeiro in Brazil. Since the building of the federal capital of Brasilia, the Pan American Highway continues on its northward course from Rio through the city of Belo Horizonte, along one of the finest stretches of motorway in the southern half of the continent, rivalling the splendours of the Caracas Autopista.

Throughout the world the vigorous expansion of tourism is proving a major source of revenue to the host countries and the importance of the Pan American Highway in this context is obvious. But there are other important benefits. The military function of the Inter-American section has been mentioned. In December 1941, following the traumatic impact of the Japanese attack on Pearl Harbor, the United States Congress author-ised $20 million to close the gaps in the road under the administration of the U.S. Bureau of Public Roads. In 1943 a further $12 million was voted for work on the extremely difficult sections in Costa Rica. The War Department also voted funds, and in 1942-3 U.S. army engineers, like their colleagues employed on the Alaskan highway, worked to open the road to Panama. The technological spin-off of war has always benefited road-building, and the effects of this highway programme on the econo-mies of the central American states in peacetime has been dramatic; in the decade from 1950 to 1960 trade in the area quadrupled.

The value of roads in South America can be demonstrated in very simple terms. It has been estimated that the cost of transport by human porters was, in 1962, about 68 cents per ton mile, by llama, about 20 cents, and by truck on the highways of the United States, about 4 cents. Official estimates in Mexico suggested that each additional kilometre of modern road added $200,000 per annum to the national product. In Peru a six-year road-building programme raised agricultural production more than six times by opening new markets. Before the building of a road between the fertile region of Caranavi in Bolivia and La Paz, the capital, the rice from this district had cost on average about 50 per cent more in the markets of the capital than rice imported from the United States; the reduction in transport costs effected by the road meant that the local producers only ninety miles away could compete effectively with the great agricultural enterprises of the north. In the case of the Caracas Autopista, the road may be said to have saved the capital from slow ex-tinction. As the crow flies the town is only ten miles from the sea, but it is over 3,000 feet above sea level and in the most mountainous terrain. Before 1950 the road was nearly nineteen miles long and even in that short distance had no fewer than 395 bends; the road was always congested, frequently blocked by rock falls and, even under the most favourable conditions, could not be traversed in under an hour. The modern four-lane freeway is about thirteen miles long and despite the switchback landscape maintains an average gradient of 1:20 and has only thirty-six bends; the journey time is down to fifteen minutes.

After several years of work on the problems presented by the terrain between Panama City and the roads of the Pan American system in Colombia, the Darien Gap sub-committee presented plans in February 1969 for the completion of the link over a distance of 250 miles within the next ten years. The proposals were the result of a radical re-examination urged on the committee by Angelo Ghiglione, formerly of the Alaskan Road Commission and thus familiar with the worst that can confront the road-builder. The route from Panama City to the frontier with Colombia presented difficulties but these were not insuperable. It was the massive barrier presented by the Atrato swamp, some twenty miles across and barring the most direct route south of the border, that had held up all work. An alternative line had been chosen that travelled south-west towards the coast and thence inland again to join the Colombian system at the town of Las Animas. But the Choco route, as it was known, was also over very difficult terrain. It called for the building of 262 miles of new road at a total estimated cost of $176 million and would have had a maximum design speed of 30 m.p.h. Ghiglione succeeded in persuading the engineering advisers of the committee to take a look at the much shorter Atrato route. The resulting proposals show how the swamp can be crossed on a twenty-five-foot embankment. This it is calculated, will sink to about half its depth, but the weight of the structure will compact the treacherous peat of the swamp sufficiently for the road to be carried. Since it is now planned to join the Colombian stretch at Rio Leon, much farther to the north, the length is only fifty miles, and the total cost of building in five projects over a ten-year period is estimated at $60 million, with allowance for a 25 per cent increase in costs built in. The road is to have a paved surface of only twenty feet in width, that is a single lane in either direction, but a design speed of 60 m.p.h. is expected. When this stretch of the great road is completed the motorist will be able to drive from the Canadian border to the capitals of the South on some of the finest highways in the world.

II

Construction of Modern Roads

MORE AND MORE people are coming to realise the extent to which the overcrowding of population and the provision of the services considered essential for modern 'civilisation' are rapidly destroying those very features of the environment itself that make life on this planet enjoyable. The kind of debate that raged round the heads of the nineteenth-century railway builders now besets the planners of airports and roads. Such transport facilities absorb valuable agricultural land or impinge on the uninterrupted vistas and rural peace which are in themselves valuable sources of recreation and relaxation to hard-pressed urban man. This question of the disfigurement of the environment is now also being seen as part of the larger and more serious problem of pollution in general. All the world's major cities are generating such a weight of fumes and industrial effluent as to endanger the very lives of their citizens. While experiments are going on to produce effective filtering systems for internal combustion engines, reliable electric motors and efficient means of silencing, the idle utopia of the computerised future is liable to be a place of pandemonium and filth to which transport will make a full contribution.

The work of the traffic engineer

If the road planner's concern for the environment is only comparatively recent, the crushing toll of accidents has prompted various attempts to improve safety. In the United States, government regulations are forcing vehicle manufacturers to ever-higher standards of safety, and since America is the world's largest market for vehicles, this is beginning to have repercussions on the industry in other countries which export to America. But road safety is determined not only by the design of the vehicles but also by that of the roads, and it is here that the expertise of the traffic engineer is called upon. His ultimate concern is safety, and to achieve the maximum degree possible for any given situation he must both plan and control—plan so as to design roads with the fewest possible traffic intersections and crossing-points, and control by regulating the flow of vehicles along the road.

Like every other aspect of modern technology this is now a highly professional and scientific discipline with an extensive literature of its own. We can nevertheless outline the basic principles. First, the aim is to minimise traffic conflict. In its most obvious form this is achieved by providing separated carriageways for up and down traffic, and multi-lane carriageways in each direction. By extending the dimensions of the road and by limiting the use of certain lanes to certain types of vehicles, so as to ensure, for example, that the outer lanes are freely available for the use of high-speed travel, it is a comparatively simple job to build an efficient road for through traffic. The real problems of the traffic engineer are caused by the perverse desire of drivers to change direction. A road without intersections and turn-offs is tidy and simple to manage but is, in effect, practically useless. Much ingenuity has been devoted to finding modes of interchange between two roads crossing one another so as to reduce to a minimum the need for changing speed or for impinging on the routes of other road-users. The classic solution is the 'clover-leaf' interchange.

Its pattern is familiar enough. Where one major route crosses another an overpass is built to carry one traffic stream over the other. Through traffic is thus virtually unimpeded while communication between the two directions is provided by a pattern of feeder roads whose lobed shape gives the intersection its name. The clover has four leaves, in fact. It also has weaknesses, the chief of which is that through traffic passes in quick succession four points at which diverting vehicles are either decelerating to leave the motorway or accelerating to join it. In either case a slight perturbation of the traffic flow is inevitable; the drivers leaving or entering the main stream are likely to force others to change their lane or at least to take account of slight deviations of movement. Compared with the decisions which are demanded minute by minute from drivers on secondary roads with unseparated two-way traffic and intersections, the pressure on the motorway driver is indeed slight, but the very quality of the road produces a new and unexpected kind of problem.

Lulled by the comparative ease of his high-speed journey, between intersections the driver finds his reflexes slowed down so that even faced with only the slightest problem he is liable to error—and at motorway speeds any kind of error can be fatal. It has been a common experience in all countries where sophisticated road systems have been introduced, that drivers, delighted by the unfamiliar freedom, have not only failed to improve their driving standards but have lapsed into astonishing carelessness. The rush of the gadarene swine along the fog-bound motorways of England is a regular feature of winter news bulletins. No kind of signalling system yet known to Man seems able to register on the mind of the Anglo-Saxon car driver once he is shrouded in the anonymity of a good thick fog. Nor is it only in Britain that the failure of drivers to come to terms with the demands of the new kind of high-speed road causes disaster; multi-vehicle pile-ups are common enough on all the world's major highway systems. While he can do nothing about the mentality of the people who use them, the road-planner is always actively seeking ways of improving the roads themselves.

Here the matter of intersections is of prime importance. Another type is the so-called catherine-wheel pattern, which makes use of an elaborate system of over- and under-passes to reduce the entrance access points to only one in each lane. A further advantage of this design is that the entrance and exit points are so arranged that the two exits precede the one entrance road. Where a freeway crosses a main road, effective and less elaborate intersection designs can be used. One of the best is the elevated roundabout where the through traffic is served by only one entrance and one exit point, and these several hundred yards apart; admittedly the traffic on the upper road has to contend with a roundabout, but even here things are not as bad as they might be. The elevated position of the roundabout ensures that traffic approaching the main road from the fast freeway below is helped to deceleration by the ramp up which it approaches the roundabout, while traffic joining the freeway from above accelerates more easily to the faster speed of the route it is entering.

Such are some of the problems and solutions of devising intersections between busy main roads, though, of course, access points to a multi-lane freeway are kept to a minimum, and minor roads that cross its course are carried over it on bridges. The number of access points and their best placing have to be carefully planned and the pattern of existing cross routes taken into account so that as far as possible they come at intervals of not less than six miles.

Landscaping the road

The construction of a major trunk road entails much more than the laying of an adequately surveyed and durable pavement. The business of fitting the road into its landscape and of providing it with an environment of its own is an important discipline and is no longer considered as a pleasant luxury. In the early eighteenth century the French department of *Ponts et*

Chaussées had included in the specifications of the new roads the requirement for the planting of trees at regular intervals, and Napoleon's engineers followed this example. In the United States during the 1920s and 1930s the term 'beautification' was applied to the scattered efforts by various official and semi-official bodies to lessen the harsh, often clumsy results of thoughtless engineering. Nowadays, however, it is recognised that the provision of shade or of decorative planting is secondary to considerations of safety. It is the story of how these 'fringe benefits' have become a central part of the road-builder's art that occupies us now.

It can plausibly be argued that the most important change in Man's everyday awareness of the world of nature is the new dimension of speed that has become the common experience of everybody in the advanced industrial nations, first through the coming of the railways, and then, with much greater impact, the spread of the motor-car. It is as much for this as for any other single reason that the design of our roads is so important. Biologically we are designed for a walking speed of three or four miles an hour; over the centuries we have become acclimatised to the slightly higher speed of horse travel, but when the standard speed of movement reaches speeds as great as 60 m.p.h. deep problems are presented and demand solutions.

The landscaping of the road depends largely on the character of the surrounding countryside for it is a basic principle that the road should look as well from the 'outside' as it does to the driver. In some contexts, for example a landscape dominated by industrial architecture such as cooling towers or mineheads and slagheaps, the road may be designed as a bold line contrasting with and offsetting its surroundings; in most cases where it passes through a rural setting it will be subordinate to it. This is particularly true in the small scale and gently rolling terrain of the English countryside. Bearing the signs of its age-long human settlement at almost every turn, this is one of the most densely detailed landscapes in the world. The roads of earlier centuries formed a natural complement to this patchwork beauty, following the natural contours and linking, like winding ribbons, one community to another. In driving his massive motorway swathes through this ever-changing scene, the modern designer has a peculiarly difficult task and must try as far as possible to subordinate the road to its surroundings.

The designer observes a number of other principles. First, all his planning is governed by the design speed. This determines a number of technical matters of construction, such as the radius of the curves and the banking of the bends, but it also shapes the landscaping of the route. The point is simply made by comparing the cases of the pedestrian walking past a gap in a hedge and a motorist driving past the same gap at a speed of, say, 60 m.p.h. For the hiker a gap of about twenty feet wide gives him something like five seconds in which to admire a distant view and to take in something of its detail; for the motorist the gap would have to be nearer 150 yards for him to enjoy the same five-second glimpse. This is one example, but the speed of travel of the observer's eye should determine every aspect of the road design.

A general consideration is the overall size and scale of the road. This can be important to the driver, who is in danger of losing sense of the speed at which he is travelling and of becoming disorientated after too long a stretch of driving on a massive six-lane highway, probably about 120 feet in width. But the matter of scale is far more important in relation to the surroundings. The actual dimensions of the carriageways are determined by the traffic that the road is designed to carry, and cannot be altered by the designer; the apparent scale of the road, however, can be modified both by the width of the central reservation and the kind of planting on it. One of the happiest solutions, and one which is often most economical in its use of land, is the spacing of the two carriageways so far from one another that the strip between them is the width of a field and available for cultivation. If such a wide distance is not possible an alternative design is to site the carriageways at different levels with well-planted trees or bushes between them. The effect of these kinds of landscaping techniques is that the driver sees only that part of the road on which he is travelling; thus the scale of the road is immediately reduced. Anyone who has driven on stretches of road like this knows how very much more interesting and enjoyable the journey is when the motorway is effectively camouflaged. The same is true for drivers on cross roads or pedestrians enjoying the countryside.

Where the road cannot be camouflaged in these ways, the builder and designer must be constantly aware of the contrast between the firm lines of the roadworks and the undulating and irregular pattern of the landscape. The point is important, both because the contrast can easily become an ugly and destructive clash in visual terms, and also because unless the strong parallels set up by the road and its attendant works and markings are counteracted, they are liable to set up a hypnotic effect on the driver. Aesthetic considerations require that the parallels be minimised as far as possible, and here aesthetics and safety go hand in hand. Parallelism is induced by such things as the edges of the carriageways, traffic-lane markings painted on the road; the tops and bottoms of the slopes and cuttings; the fences and such other elements. Some of these things can obviously not be modified but other things such as the level of the slopes can be and, when well designed, can reduce the parallel effect. As far as possible the height of the slopes should be varied and well rounded, so that a good fence line can be established close to the road where the cuttings are steep, swinging out where the land levels out. However, the line should follow the contour of the slopes. Far from adding interest, a line swinging in and out from the road on perfectly flat country is simply an irritant.

The fourth major element in road landscaping is the design of the bridges. Again the determining factor is the speed of the observer, and the designer has to work to a scale of miles of roadway as the unit. For this reason, on a stretch traversed by a number of crossroads, the bridges should be designed as a series rather than as individual structures, and since they are approached at high speed the texture, although important as the bridge is viewed from the side of the motorway, is less significant than the shape.

These, then, are some of the general principles behind the landscaping of motor roads and nowhere are they more seriously applied than in the United States. There the decline in accident rates, from 16 deaths per 100 million vehicle miles during the 1920s to only 6·4 in the 1950s, may be attributed among other causes to the improved design of the highways offering the driver a more interesting and stimulating journey and thus keeping him more generally alert. In 1958 a Bill was passed to limit the amount of roadside advertising on the main trunk routes—a further important step in the direction of road safety. It is now generally accepted that 'aesthetic' considerations are central in the planning of a new road and, where engineering and economic factors balance one another out, they may be decisive.

An outstanding example of expert landscaping coupled with good engineering is the Garden State Parkway in New Jersey, which is 173 miles long and runs from the north of the state to the southern resort of Cape May. It was completed in 1956 at a total cost of more than $300 million, and of this total the New Jersey Authority estimated only $10 million were added by the decision to landscape. The result is considered to be one of the safest and most beautiful roads in America. Care was, of course, taken to keep costs down wherever possible and, following this aim, some of the stretches were laid through country already wooded, thus limiting the need for further planting. Elsewhere trees and shrubs were used to stabilise steep slopes and also to blend bridge structures into their surroundings. In the country stretches the central reservation is between twenty-four and thirty-four feet in width and is occupied by a raised mound, to cut down headlamp glare, planted with creeper to save maintenance costs. On the lengths that run through urban districts and cannot therefore have such a wide central reservation (at times it is as little as ten feet) a baffle fence was erected and climbing plants trained against it to reduce the danger of monotony.

The survey

It is the traffic engineer who lays down the functional specifications for
the road; the volume of traffic that it is to carry, the speed that is expected
on it, the minimum headroom clearance for bridges carrying minor roads
over the freeway; and the minimum clearances between the piers of the
bridges and the traffic lanes. Other matters to be decided by the traffic
engineer include the specifications for gradients and curvatures of bends.
Most modern motorways, for example, have maximum gradients of
between 1 in 30 and 1 in 34 (exactly comparable with the governing
gradient on Telford's London-to-Holyhead road) and a minimum radius
of 900 metres for curves. Finally it is the traffic engineer's job to specify
the width of the carriageway, the width of the central reservation and the
distance of uninterrupted visibility, based on the driver's eye-level in
the average passenger car, along the road.

  Thus, even before the surveyors have begun to plan the route across
the countryside, they have a large body of specifications to bear in mind.
It is their job to find the route that will most cheaply, most directly and
with the least inconvenience to existing roads, take the freeway along its
intended course. Compared with his Roman predecessors, the modern
road surveyor has an unenviable task. It must be admitted that the
Roman surveyor had frequently to work in fear of enemy attack, since he
was often working over recently 'pacified' territory, but he could at least
rely for protection on the finest fighting-men the world had seen. (There
must be many occasions when his modern equivalent, hedged about by
specifications and Ministry regulations, would welcome a stand-up fight
as a safety valve for frayed nerves.) Furthermore, however infested
it may have been by bandits and resistance fighters, the terrain over
which the Roman surveyor had to work was free of land-owning problems
and numerous built-up areas.

  Considerations for the beauty of the landscape, now of increasing
importance, could also be disregarded by these earlier engineers if only
because the vested interests of the ancient Britons in their local beauty
spots could hardly have been of much concern to the Roman military
authorities. Also, of course, the dimensions and requirements of the finest
Roman roads bore no comparison to the vast swathes of precious land
devoured by a modern freeway.

  In addition to such considerations of amenity, the surveyor has also
an obligation to recommend the most economical route. While meeting
the specifications of the traffic engineers, it should also ensure the minimum of earth-moving, one of the most expensive of all the operations
involved in the building of a major road. The road will lie over hilly
country, so that as far as possible the 'cut' (the earth excavated) should

balance the 'fill' (the earth required for embankments). The shifting of too great a surplus, one that cannot be legitimately incorporated in landscaping features, or the transportation of large quantities of earth to make up any 'shortfall', can ruin the economic viability of the whole project. The cost of moving earth is so high that occasionally, when the road must traverse a deep valley and yet maintain an even gradient, a viaduct carrying the whole six-lane highway may well be cheaper than an embankment. It is a measure of the advance in modern civil engineering that this type of exercise, which far exceeds in sheer dimensions many of the achievements of the heroic age of nineteenth-century railway building, evokes none of the public enthusiasm and admiration which greeted the doings of Brunel or Brassey.

The surveying of a road is done in five phases. First comes the reconnaissance of the ground both with the map and also in the field to decide on the general route; this is followed by the selection of a number of possible routes and the isolation of the best locations; then comes the preliminary survey, now usually aerial, from which is built a topographic strip map of the two or three routes selected. The fourth stage is the projection on to the strip map so as to fit the detail to the actual earth surface as closely as possible while adhering to the geometric characteristics of the specification (at this stage matters of landscaping and the economies of cut and fill are of decisive importance). Finally comes what is called the location survey, which is simply the transferring of the elements on the map on to the ground preparatory to the start of excavations. One of the first steps after the surveyed route has been decided is the sending out of advance parties of engineers to begin work on the bridges and tunnels along the route; concurrently with this the preparation of soil and drainage begins.

Construction

From work on the virgin soil to the day of the ceremonial opening, the building of a modern road is now a matter of largely mechanised routine. First the top soil is removed by a scraper with sharp cutting teeth. This is followed by a bulldozer that shifts the loosened soil to one side, so that along its whole length the road bed is flanked by piles of soil ready to be used at the end of the main works for landscaping the verges and the central reservation. After the general line of the road has been stripped in this way, it is cut and shaped to the levels and curvatures set down in the traffic engineer's specifications, excavations and embankments being made to balance out as far as possible. This is the most expensive phase of the whole operation. The equipment is extremely expensive both to hire and to run, and demands the most efficient possible deployment of the variety of excavators and earth-moving machines used. For this reason it is of great advantage that any national or regional road-building programme should as far as possible be co-ordinated, to allow the equipment and the teams that operate it to move from one project to another so that they can build up a tradition of expertise and work as a team.

The depth to which the subsoil is cut depends largely on the type of road bed to be used; this may consist of crushed rocks laid on the subsoil or of the subsoil itself specially treated to give a weight-bearing foundation. If rock is to be used, the soil must be excavated to a depth of about two feet below the planned final level of the road. Another type of foundation is a layer of very coarse concrete, but perhaps the simplest method is that of soil stabilisation. This is only possible where the characteristic of the soil is suitable to treatment, and determining this is a branch of the science of soil mechanics.

The best results in soil stabilisation are obtained from a well-graded soil, with a uniform distribution of gravel, sand and clay types. If soil stabilisation has been decided upon the first step is to loosen the subsoil to a depth of between one and two feet; next a binding agent is mixed with the soil; the mixture is watered, tamped down, rolled thoroughly and, when hard, covered with a waterproof top surface. These various operations have become standardised and can be all carried out by a number of machines, the most sophisticated of which can do the whole operation, from turning the subsoil to rolling the resultant 'soil cement'.

A large machine of this type may work at a speed as high as thirty to thirty-five feet per minute, laying a soil cement road bed twelve feet wide and one foot six inches deep. The best soil for this treatment is the well-graded type described above, but soils of uniform grading, i.e. sand or gravel, can also be treated and desert roads will usually have a foundation of soil cement. A soil which is unevenly 'graded' is prone to air pockets between the particles and the likelihood of a high water content, and cannot be adequately treated, so alternative foundations must be laid.

After the foundation, or footing as it is sometimes called, has been prepared, next comes the base course, either of asphaltic concrete or so-called 'lean' concrete. On top of this is laid the pavement which again may be of asphalt, 'black top' paving or concrete. It is at this stage that the mechanisation of modern road-building is at its most impressive.

The most advanced type of road-making equipment, first developed in the United States and now commonly used on the new roads of Europe, is a single, self-powered machine called a 'slip-form' paver. It performs all the operations necessary to convert wet mixed concrete, fed into it as it slowly advances, into a complete concrete slab. It moves at a speed of about six feet per minute on its own caterpillar tracks and the concrete is so firmly compacted when it emerges that there is no need for wooden 'forms' to support the sides of the pavement while the concrete sets. Such machines are capable of producing a road surface of about twenty-five feet in width and one foot deep, and subsequent improvements have made it possible to use the machine to produce a reinforced pavement. The steel-mesh webs are suspended at the required height ahead of the paver which passes over them, forcing the concrete through the mesh and compacting it in position by means of vibrators.

Another method of laying down a concrete road surface allots the various functions to a number of machines. These move along the prepared foundations on tracks whose inner edges constitute the 'form' containing the concrete as it sets. This moving assembly line typically consists of four machines. The first is a spreader, which lays out the base layer of concrete; this is followed by a mobile crane outside the track, which lays the reinforcing mesh steel on the setting concrete. Then comes another spreader which lays the surface layer, and behind this a vibrator that compacts the concrete. The final surface is provided by a finishing machine which ensures the correct camber on the surface for drainage purposes and also lightly scores the surface to give a skid-proof finish.

Although these machines are able to provide a completely continuous flow of concrete, the engineer must nevertheless build into the finished road a number of joints to guard against the expansion of the finished road surface in extreme heat and to control the inevitable slight fissuring of the surface formed by the contraction of the concrete as it sets. The expansion joints are formed by narrow strips set upright in grooves spanning the whole width of the pavement and placed in position before the first layer of concrete is laid. The strips are of a material that can accept a certain degree of compression, and rise to within about an inch of the upper surface of the finished roadway. They are topped by a coping that is removed when the concrete has set. The grooves in the road surface thus formed are then cleaned out and sealed with a resilient waterproofing compound so as to leave an uninterrupted surface. The contraction joints, which travel both across and along the direction of the road, are formed by laying narrow strips in the hardening concrete and do not extend downwards more than about 25 per cent of the depth of the pavement. When the surface has hardened these strips are also removed and the grooves filled with a sealer. By this means the cracks that can be expected in the drying concrete are largely under the builder's control and the dangers of water and ice settling and disrupting the road surface minimised.

Ideally, the expensive and complicated operation equipment should be at work non-stop both to maximise its use and also to take advantage of its ability to provide an uninterrupted flow of material. Sometimes, indeed, the building operation may continue at night under flood-lighting, but more often work stops and various types of 'construction' joints are used to provide the link between the two day's workings. Such joints are often strengthened by short steel dowels projecting horizontally from the finished slab fitting into collars in the next slab; in this way heat expansion in the finished road surface is allowed for. The machinery and techniques described for concrete surfaces are used, with slight modifications, for the laying of asphalt and in both cases have immensely improved the speed and efficiency with which cross-country freeways can be constructed. For new major roads in built-up areas where the roads are often carried over the city on elevated carriageways, completely different methods of construction are needed.

Urban motorways

First used in America, the elevated urban motorway is now a common enough sight in all the world's major cities, from London to Tokyo. It is probably the most obvious visual symbol of the transformation of city life in the modern age.

As more and more roads 'take to the air', and the roar of fast-moving traffic throbs outside the first-floor windows of houses and offices, the old sense of the city as a centre where all roads converge and from which the fertilising ideals of civilisation emerge, is destroyed. The revolution launched with the mass production of the motor-car at the beginning of this century is by no means finished. Perhaps the single most important agent in the changing of traditional ideas about men and society, the car is now in the process of destroying the roots and stem of the European type of civilisation based on the city. For the mobility that the motor-car offers to all members of an advanced industrial society is a vital element in the levelling of hierarchy and social class. Equally the concentration of commerce, culture and administration in city complexes is being diffused by the easy access that communications of all kinds give to remote and previously backward areas.

The problem of providing for increased traffic flow through already over-congested city streets is being met in a variety of ways. The first and most obvious is the fullest possible exploitation of existing roads. One-way systems and diversionary routes are set up to take traffic off the overcrowded main thoroughfares on to less frequented side streets. But this is only a stop-gap to ease the worst effects of street plans developed in earlier times for less heavy traffic densities.

Somewhat more permanent measures are represented by urban tunnels, such as those taking through traffic under Brussels and Paris, but more common and less expensive than these are the elevated urban freeways. Here are some of the most dramatic signs of the contemporary cityscape's destructive effect on once well-loved localities. Since the prime reason of these high-level expressways and the aptly named flyovers is to avoid the congestion beneath, the first objective must be to reduce the area of the surrounding columns to the minimum. In Japan, where the world of the present is habitually on terms of easy familiarity with the beauties of the past, the historic capital of Tokyo is traversed by expressways which, at points, produce three levels of high-speed traffic one above the other.

One such road is the Expressway Route Number 4, linking the Olympic stadium with the Haneda International Airport. For most of its length the road is some forty-five feet wide, having two lanes in both directions, and the road surface consists of reinforced concrete six inches deep supported on hollow steel columns. The substructure of the road is formed by twin box-steel girders and a steel lattice-work supported on a double row of steel columns. Where the roadway forks it is carried on a central single row of these columns with the road cantilevered out on either side. The cantilever principle is used on many other urban freeways, and the material used is frequently prestressed concrete.

Where the elevated road is to be of considerable length the constructional problems are correspondingly more complex. The first stage after the foundations have been prepared is the erection of the concrete pillars that are to carry the highway. The roadway substructure consists of prefabricated, prestressed concrete sections, the width of the roadway and about six feet in length; each span between the supporting pillars is set up, section by section, on a wooden staging or scaffolding. The hollow sections are given the required rigidity by tensioning them with cables that run through them in an undulating pattern along the direction of the road. As each span is put in place the staging is dismantled and moved on ready for the next.

The result of such a building technique is a highly sophisticated structure in which rigidity is obtained by the high tension of the internal cables. The point of support between the bottom of the road substructure and the top of the columns is on sliding bearings that permit expansion or contraction in the road as it is caused by temperature changes, and also a small degree of rotation to allow for occasional structural distortions resulting from heavy or ill-balanced traffic flow. Thus, despite the massive loads that the road carries and the speeds at which these are moving, the whole fabric depends on bearing elements that are neither rigid in themselves nor fixed in their seatings.

12

Road Administration
and Finance

THE IMPORTANCE OF roads in national development plans and their wide ramifications in national planning have become apparent. In this chapter we look at the departments that administer the road programmes in various parts of the world and the way in which the programmes themselves are financed, concentrating our attention on developments in post-war Britain. We shall also describe some of the general principles behind road pricing.

In every advanced country roads now occupy an increasingly high place in national priorities, but the pattern of their central administration is often the result of age-old historical developments. In France, for example, the long tradition of central responsibility for the trunk routes is maintained by an élite group of highway engineers of the *Corps des Ingénieurs des Ponts et Chaussées*. Unlike the engineers recruited to the British Ministry of Transport, men who have enjoyed high professional status but are withdrawn from the practical business of road-building, the French technocrats of the road have direct involvement in and responsibility for design and construction.

Britain

Britain's system is no less a reflection of the national tradition of government. In roads, as in education and many other vital aspects of social policy, responsibility is divided between the centre and a strong substructure of local authorities. The two sections are so closely interlocked that it has been said that reform in the field of urban road-building is inseparable from reform of local government itself. The intimate correlation between roads and the communities they serve could hardly be more forcibly expressed, but in the face of modern developments the British system of shared responsibility has been gradually modified in the second half of the twentieth century so that the centre has unmistakably become the dominant partner.

Before the reforms proposed in the 1969 Royal Commission on Local Government there were no fewer than 823 authorities responsible in some way for roads, while forty-two county authorities were involved in the national motorway programme. Up to the 1950s the national investment in roads was so meagre (little more than £10 million per year) that the programme hardly merited major administrative reform. But between 1955 and the late 1960s the amount spent on new roads or major improvements of existing roads increased from £13 million to £300 million, and the necessity of controlling capital investment of this size made a review of the administrative structure imperative.

As heirs to a century-long tradition, however, local authorities jealously guard their powers. Overnight change is out of the question, though evolution to a more centralised system was remarkably rapid in the late 1960s. The main clashes of interest between regional and central governments is in finance and supervision. In the case of trunk routes and motorways, for example, the Ministry has provided the money but has used the personnel, both administrative and engineering, of local authorities in the design and supervision of the work. Other roads are the direct responsibility of local authorities, but in many cases they are subsidised by the central administration, which thus has a certain amount of control over the programme.

The links between local and central government are numerous and close; there is plenty of scope for inefficiency and administrative confusion, but the situation is particularly damaging in the area of urban motorways. In its evidence to the Commission on Local Government the Ministry pointed out that 'it is in the provincial conurbations that the present structure of local government is most defective for highway planning'. Among such conurbations are Merseyside, 'Selnec'—South East Lancashire and North East Cheshire—the West Riding of Yorkshire and Tyneside.

At this time the Ministry complained:

> The difficulties of integrating highway planning with the general planning of the country are most vividly illustrated by the disputes which frequently arise in connection with the control of development that affects roads or land reserved for future roads. Jurisdiction over planning applications is frequently delegated to lower-tier authorities which have no major highway responsibilities. Such a multiplicity of

planning jurisdictions and the divorce of highway planning responsibilities has obvious and serious dangers for the planning of major
roads.

A step towards the co-ordination of national and local interests was
taken by the Labour Government in forming a Secretaryship of State
for Local Government and Regional Planning, with overriding responsibility for Housing and Transport. Their Tory successors established the
first Ministry for the Environment. However, this apparent advance
seemed to be nullified by the fact that the first Minister had already, in a
previous post, approved two developments opposed both by local opinion
and expert reports on the grounds of being detrimental to the environment. Governments will have to take threats to the environment seriously
and it must be admitted that roads constitute such a threat.

A more immediate move towards rational administration was the
setting up in the mid-1960s of six Road Construction Units, with responsibility between them for all English motorway and trunk-road
schemes costing more than £1 million. Thus the inter-urban road programme moved to a greater degree of centralisation. The Road Construction Units were charged with responsibility over a wide field, including
the scheduling of schemes, the acquisition of land for rights of way and
the letting of contracts to construction companies. They represented a
reasonable compromise between the need for decentralisation in detailed
matters of work in progress and the need for central decision on questions
of general policy and finance, both of which remained with the Ministry.

This element of compromise, so often regarded as the hallmark of
British governmental practice, was extended still further to provide a
bridge between the old system of county control and the new more
centralised organisation. The Road Construction Units themselves have
sub-units based in county council offices and often using county council
employees, seconded to this function of trunk-road administration under
the direction of a national body. No doubt the trend in the future will be
towards greater centralisation but the kind of solution outlined here
represents an intelligent approach to the problem of loosening the age-
old hold of the localities over transport systems now regarded as a national
service.

But the R.C.U.s are not merely an administrative improvement; they
are valuable also in raising the status of Ministry engineers who now have
direct responsibility for construction jobs in the field. A similar improvement was made in the status of the ten Divisional Road Engineers who
for more than a century have provided the main point of liaison between
the central and local authorities. Their status, threatened by the new
structure of R.C.U.s, was to some extent restored by the increase in their

responsibilities. They now have full engineering responsibility for schemes costing up to £1 million and financial responsibility for schemes up to a quarter of that figure.

In France engineers in government employ have always enjoyed high professional respect and active participation in the practical business of construction. In England, with a strict and traditional division between general administration and specialised technical expertise, and with the former the more highly regarded, the engineer has had to become an administrator if he hoped to rise in the Service. In most sections of the British Civil Service the system still obtains. In the Highways section of the Ministry of Transport, however, although there was a transition period in which some sections had two heads, one of them 'administrative' the other 'engineering', there is now an integrated chain of command headed by a Director-General of Highways who at the time of writing is in fact an engineer.

Road-pricing

In addition to administrators and engineers, the Ministry of Transport, like any other modern department of roads, has also to enlist the services of many other experts. Among them are professional economists whose job is the evaluation and cost analysis of alternative road schemes, and cost estimation and forward planning of the national road system as a whole. The main factors to be taken into consideration are the cost of *not* having an improved road, measured in journey times and accident rates; the comparative vehicle running costs; and the return on capital investment.

Cost-benefit analysis, when applied to roads, presents a number of unique difficulties for it must take into account not merely measurable items, such as construction and land acquisition, but also others which, by their nature, are much less precise. The building of a new road may yield obvious advantages in terms of faster journey times and cheaper transport, but it may also destroy the amenities of a rural or urban area important as a beauty spot, historical landmark or for recreation. Furthermore, it may be questioned whether the savings produced by good roads in terms of transport costs can be considered as a true monetary return in the same sense as the income yield by more conventionally understood types of investment. Finally, the very value of the existing investment represented by the nation's road system is far from obvious.

Clearly, the actual historic cost is very different from the replacement cost. It has been estimated that the total replacement cost of the British national road system amounts to some £3,000 million and that the cost of road developments envisaged for the 1970s and 1980s amounts to about

£2,000 million. For a country planning to increase its road investment by some 60 per cent in the near future, the need for a streamlined central administration is becoming increasingly obvious. Indeed, there would seem to be a good case for a separate national road board charged with long-term development.

The problem of costing roads has been alluded to, and parallel to it is the vexed question of paying for them. The money collected from road users in taxes on vehicle registrations and fuel, as well as driving-licence fees, often far exceeds the amount expended on road-building and improvements. The facts seem to be clear and the complaints are vociferous. But on reflection it is equally clear that the cost to the community in terms of atmospheric pollution and disturbance of amenities may well be far higher. The disposition of national income is a political question and involves the community in the expression of priorities through the political process.

More relevant to the student of transport is the cost that the road-user imposes on himself in terms of congestion by the excessive intensive use of the limited facilities available in built-up urban areas. Faced with the spiralling problem of congestion, economists and others are concerning themselves with the development of road-pricing systems that will enable the costs to be met by the road users themselves. The aim is to find a method of pricing and payment that will reflect accurately the costs involved, will encourage the best use of existing roads, indicate where they need improvement and raise funds for that improvement.

There are two distinct elements here. First is the cost of providing the roads. This comprises the costs of construction, estimated on a forty-year period of amortisation; maintenance, which includes repairs, the provision of ancillary facilities such as signposting, lighting, policing, administration, cleansing and snow clearance; land acquisition; and finally the interest on the capital raised to meet all these costs. Secondly, there is the cost of using the roads. This comprises the wear and tear on the vehicles, congestion costs and the community costs already referred to. Pricing is of two main types related to quite distinct types of road— the urban and the rural motorway. In the former case, road-pricing is considered primarily as a punitive and regulatory measure designed to reduce the number of vehicles and thus limit congestion. In the latter case the aim is, more generally, to recoup from the users the expense of providing the road.

Various types of tolls have been collected with success in Japan, Italy, the United States and other parts of the world; they have had only very limited application in Britain, however, being levied over short distances and for the upkeep of specific utilities such as bridges and tunnels. Their use on motorways has been opposed since it is claimed that the access points on a British motorway are too numerous to make toll-gates economic. It is also feared that levying tolls on the new roads would be counterproductive, since it might drive traffic back on to the poorer roads.

Perhaps the real reason behind the British reluctance to resort to tolls lies elsewhere: in the public belief that for the last fifty years successive governments have misappropriated road taxes for almost any purpose but road improvement. What Minister of Transport would dare impose charges for the use of the few hundred miles of motorways now being tardily built? But however unsatisfactory the state of British roads for modern traffic conditions, there are few countries in the world that have a more extensive network, in relation to land area, of metalled roads and alternative routes. Despite the high quality of her modern road programme, for instance, Japan is not otherwise well provided and in many instances the modern toll road is unavoidable; while in Italy the success of the toll roads rests heavily on tourist traffic, usually unfamiliar with the country and more interested in speed than economy.

The problems of levying tolls on motorways are slight, however, when compared with those of charging for travel in any great urban centre. Nevertheless, congestion is becoming such a pressing problem that techniques are being evolved. Underlying thinking in this field is the concept of the optimal economic capacity of any road system. The traffic flow in congested streets tends to stabilise at the point where the road cost for those who find it just worth their while to join the traffic stream, equals the benefits that they obtain from their journeys.

A primitive system of road-pricing, in the shape of parking charges, already exists in many large cities but the only tax on movement of vehicles is the fuel tax. Of the various methods for levying a toll one of the most promising is a static electricity cell installed on the vehicle, possibly on the number plate. The capacity of the cell is depleted by a measured amount when it passes over a wire carrying a low electric current. When the meter is exhausted it registers this by a colour change; the driver then simply buys a new meter or has his existing one recharged.

The British motorway programme

Britain was one of the last of the world's major industrial countries to embark on a motorway programme. This can partly be explained by the fact that she had one of the most comprehensive networks of roads and was therefore less absolutely in need of new routes, and partly because the general level of maintenance over this large network was relatively good. The other side of the coin is, of course, the seemingly chronic lethargy of the British administrative process.

After the short burst of activity at the beginning of the nineteenth century there was a great lull in road-building as the energies of the whole nation, or so it seemed, were engrossed by the railway—the *modern*, nineteenth-century, mode of transport. In the last two decades of the century, however, a new craze swept society and the bicycle became the essential vehicle for the Victorian whizz-kid. And it was the cyclists in Britain, as in the United States, who were among the most vocal advocates of better roads. In 1886 the bicycle 'lobby' founded the Road Improvement Association and the campaign gathered strength in the new century. In the 1910s the Government founded the Road Board which was empowered to build roads primarily for motor traffic. None were built, however, and in the 1920s the raids on the road tax, that were to become all too familiar, began. It was Winston Churchill, as Chancellor of the Exchequer, who first drew on this source both to finance government spending and also, it has been suggested, to protect the already declining fortunes of the railways.

In 1937 government road financing in Britain became the object of an annual grant. This was always too small and made planning for the future more or less meaningless. In the immediate post-war period the reforming Socialist Government turned its attention to roads and by the Trunk Roads Act of 1946 made 3,685 miles of main highways the responsibility of the Ministry of Transport. At last, in 1949, the Special Roads Act officially recognised the principle of the Motorway, a principle that had, in fact, first been mooted in England and that as early as 1910 in Sidney Webb's book *The King's Highway*. Finally in 1959, after an unseemly rush in which production schedules were forced to political deadlines, the first stretch of Britain's first motorway was opened to the public. For a variety of reasons, some less respectable than others, the M1 proved to have more than its fair share of teething troubles, but the process of bringing Britain's roads up to date had got off to a start, if a belated one.

In the same year the modernisation of the Great North Road, the A1, began and three years later most of the route from County Durham to London had been converted to dual carriageway. Work also began on the Firth of Forth road bridge, and in the ensuing years others were built, notably the Tamar bridge linking Plymouth to Cornwall at Saltash, and the great work over the Severn which, by virtue of its aerofoil design, was one of the most revolutionary suspension bridges in the world. The year 1959 saw the first 'clearway' experiments on British roads, which, by prohibiting stopping on certain main urban routes, made possible improved traffic speeds without structural alterations.

Expenditure on road-building and improvement began to approach realistic proportions as the 1960s progressed—from £44,024,000 for the year 1958–9, to an estimated £225,100,000 for 1968–9. The actual

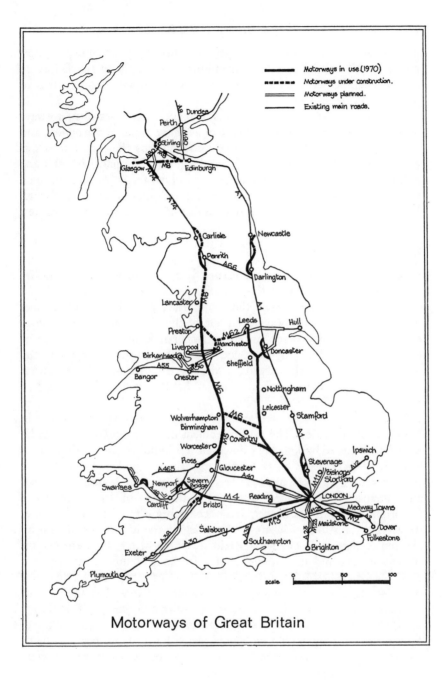

Motorways of Great Britain

increase should have been still larger, but from 1965 actual expenditure began to fall behind planned expenditure due partly to the failure to complete all the necessary statutory procedures required before new road schemes can be implemented.

However, by April 1969 there was a total of 604 miles of motorways open in Britain, while a further 265 miles were under construction, and it seemed probable that the target of 1,000 miles by the end of 1972 was well in sight. When this target is reached, and the final planned 1,400 miles of motorway are completed, Britain in the mid-1970s will still be a long way behind Western Germany, Europe's leader in this field, though her record will not compare badly with that of other European countries.

Motorways in London

Most of this book has been concerned with long-distance roads rather than city streets. Not until the last fifty years have the latter produced any real problems other than those of surfacing, drainage and sewage. Traffic, or course, has always been one of the disadvantages of city life; complaints against it were voiced in Imperial Rome and seventeenth-century London, but only now does the danger present a threat to the organic structure of the city itself and force us to ask ourselves what we expect of city life and what values we hold more highly than the free movement of traffic.

Put like this, the matter seems simple, even to those who do not live in the heart of our cities. The traffic problem in any conurbation could be solved very easily by knocking down all the buildings and laying a network of roads on the site. But, of course, there would be no traffic, for traffic results from social needs and requirements; from homes, businesses and cinemas. Clearly, then, traffic is a function of something more important, many things in fact, and once we begin to ask what these are, we are in a position to debate to what degree traffic facilities should be allowed to detract from them. Might it not be better to accept certain inconveniences and inhibitions on our freedom of movement between attractive or profitable destinations in order to preserve the very qualities of those destinations themselves? It seems unlikely that the cult of 'efficiency', defined as it is on the most restricted criterion of monetary profit, has yet reached the point where the physical demolition of, say, Westminster Abbey, would be contemplated by road-planners. Even in monetary terms such a demolition would be counterproductive in view of the growing importance of tourism. There are, then, some limits to our willingness to accommodate traffic.

The motorway plan for London would, on the lowest estimate, however, involve the demolition of 19,600 houses and the displacement of some

60,000 people, the destruction of many of the more pleasant of London's residential districts, which contribute to its character as a city, and the disruption of the lives of hundreds of thousands of its citizens. It has been estimated that, when the plan is completed, about one million people will be living within 200 yards of a motorway; many are already living in much closer proximity to existing elevated motorways, with consequent nightmares of noise, fumes and the deterioration of their property (*see* Plate 26).

The main proposals are for three ring-roads. The first, at between three and four miles from the centre, will have a length of thirty miles; the second, at about seven miles from the centre, is to be fifty miles; the third will be about 100 miles in length, and outside this again there is to be an outer orbital road which, if built, would pass through parts of the green belt. In addition there are to be twelve radial motorways bringing traffic close into the heart of the city or on to the ring-roads themselves. The proposals also recognise the necessity for improvements to the existing system of secondary roads.

In his excellent book *Motorways in London*, the fruits of a working party of the London Amenity and Transport Association, which he led, J. Michael Thomson has listed many of the objections to be made to the plan in its present form. His most important point concerns the strategy of highway planning: even where a demand for transport facilities exists and may well be increasing we, as a society, are free either to meet or to restrain that demand. In other words, as observed above, it may be decided that there are more important things than unrestrained mobility. Further, 'The process of providing more and more capacity, with little regard to the economic or social cost, in order to meet the growing pressure of uncontrolled demand, is not likely to solve the problem but rather to reproduce the same problem on a larger scale.' The capacity of roads for generating traffic has been proved again and again in American cities, and some leading American cities are now resorting to heavy investment in public transport systems. Yet it seems that London's own authority is at the moment preparing a scarred but still splendid city as a sacrificial victim on the altar of automania.

To the Londoner himself the motorways will be of slight advantage. The vast majority of journeys within the city, being less than five miles, will still be largely on the existing network and, since almost all journeys start on local or secondary routes, the new traffic generated by the motorways will lead to further congestion of those routes as well as a diminution in the average speeds on the motorways themselves. Thus, although some of the through traffic will be taken off the existing network, more will be generated and the situation will be only slightly improved. The plan will cost an estimated £1,100 million. Yet this sum takes no account of

compensation for thousands of families; no account of the social responsibility or otherwise of demolishing close on 20,000 adequate houses in a
city where already an estimated quarter of a million people are awaiting
new ones; and, most surprisingly of all, it does not take into account the
cost of the improvements acknowledged as necessary if the existing system
is to serve the new routes. It is estimated that by 1981 all the access roads
to Ringway 1 will be overloaded.

The full critique of London's proposed motorway plan is much more
damaging than we have space to show here, but a general conclusion
seems unavoidable. If road-planning for our major cities starts with the
assumption that, as far as possible, projected traffic demand must be
accommodated, then we must accept that the cities themselves will be
killed. The towns of Europe grew to facilitate the processes of trade, and
still the amenities they provide for rapid money-making are the chief
cause of their being, yet over the centuries they have become something
more than markets. In seeking solutions to the vast problem of transport
within urban areas, the people who live in them must have a determining
voice. The communities must decide whether they value the excitements
and pleasures of an urban culture more than the privilege of absolute
freedom of movement for privately owned vehicles.

In our age the history of the road has for the first time become a determining factor in the history of society. It is clear that the car has changed
society, and is continuing to do so, but we are still able to influence the
change. It is up to us to exercise our option.

13

The Future of Transport

BEFORE THIS CENTURY is out developments in transport and communications may well have robbed the road of many of its traditional functions. We are now concerned with trends in the technologically more advanced countries, but these are also indications for the world as a whole in a still more distant future. One further qualification must also be made. What is even now technically feasible cannot be expected to become general for some years. Throughout the world the capital investment in conventional roads and conventional methods of transport is too immense to be dispensed with overnight. Plans are still being laid for future highways and motorways designed to serve the type of vehicle common today, so although the internal combustion engine will gradually be displaced, it will remain for certain uses into the next century.

Our glimpse into the future is of necessity based to some extent on our knowledge of the past. Up to the beginning of the railway age, roads had served three basic functions: the transport of people, freight and information. By the end of the nineteenth century the railways had taken much passenger and freight traffic from their ancient rivals, and the bulk of the postal services of all advanced countries was carried by rail. In our own century, for reasons touched on in an earlier chapter, a large proportion of freight and passenger traffic has returned to the roads, while telecommunications have provided a new vehicle for the transmission of much information that had previously been carried by the post. In this century, too, transport, in common with all the services of civilised communities, is being violently complicated by an increase in the world's population. By the end of the century this will have doubled and, still more significant for our purposes, the number of people living in urban areas will have quadrupled.

If the present pattern of living out of town and working in the centre continues, the problems of commuter transport will become virtually unmanageable. Already great conurbations such as Tokyo, New York and London are facing desperate difficulties—so desperate that even slight variations in the weather are sufficient to bring train services to a halt and make roads impassable. In the future, however, the advanced use of computers and telecommunications may mean that many people will have no need to go to an 'office' at all. They will be linked to all the necessary services by telephone lines. If such a pattern became general, obviously the pressure on the roads would be eased. However, this would merely slow down, rather than reverse, a trend to increasing use, and other factors will be of more importance in altering the nature of overland transport.

In the first place more and more types of freight will leave the road and take to totally new methods of transportation. Already one of the principal items of freight overland, fuel, has been increasingly diverted. Electricity is carried by power-lines, gas by pipelines. Now advances are being made in the transport of solids, such as coal even, by pipeline. The solid is pulverised and placed in suspension in some liquid solution which may be able to carry more than one type of 'slurry'; this is pumped from the source of supply to the consumer and there separated out from its liquid transporter. It is possible by this means that techniques will be devised for using crude oil, at present distributed over large areas of the globe by pipeline, as a carrier of other raw materials.

Other forms of tube transport are also under active consideration. In one the material is conveyed in its solid state in containers but these, rather than riding on a road or railway, are shuttled through tightly fitting but low-friction tubes, probably made of variants of glass fibre. The train of such containers, which could also be suited to the carriage of passengers as well as freight, will be supported not on wheels but on a cushion of moving air which will also provide the motive power. The principle of these so called Pneumatic Logictubes depends on the difference in air pressure behind the 'train' and in front of it. A system of low-pressure blowers feeds air in behind and extracts it from in front, while the continuous moving cushion of air beneath it eliminates friction almost completely.

An early form of the system was developed at the Institut Battelle of Geneva in the late 1960s, and has already been used for the transport of goods. Such tubes will be either above or below ground. In the case of passenger transport, the above-ground tube, constructed of transparent glass fibre and conveying trains of a similar transparent fibre, will give the travellers a unique and uninterrupted view of the countryside.

In the area of long-distance passenger transport the road will also experience increasing competition from the railway, making its comeback on the basis of vastly increased speeds. Already, the famous Japanese train along the historic Tokaido 'strip' carries commuter traffic at speeds of over 125 miles an hour. In the 1970s we can expect turbine trains, already operating in Canada, to be general in the United States, France, the United Kingdom and the Soviet Union, travelling faster than 155 miles an hour.

For shorter journeys involving mass transportation, various forms of continuously moving pavements will become general. A small and primitive version of this principle is already in use on London Transport, linking Bank and Monument Underground stations. But this is only the prelude to a far more ambitious system called the H.V.C.S. or High Volume Continuous System. This is expected to be general in all sizeable conurbations by the year 2000, all 'private cars' having been banned from city centres. It is estimated that a continuously moving pavement, travelling at a peak speed of some 9 m.p.h., but with access points about every 500 yards for the pedestrian to get on at standard walking speed, will save him about ten minutes per mile, and the community some £80,000 per day at fare rates then obtaining. Indeed, a British architect, Brian Richards, has estimated that the running costs of such a transport mode would be between ten and twenty times less than any other over the distance. These estimates are based on the conventional roller-belt transmission systems as used at present. But the air-cushion principle is also applicable here, and this would reduce still further the elements of friction and tension in the belt, allowing it to be of material lighter in weight and cheaper.

For longer distances, plans have been described for the replacement of the underground train and above-ground bus services with a continuous transporter travelling at between 20 and 25 m.p.h. The aim of the designers is to eliminate time-consuming stops at stations, and also to put an end to the present wasteful use of the capital investment, more than half of which is represented by the tunnels themselves. It has been calculated that even at the height of peak rush-hour travel more than 80 per cent of the tunnels are empty as the result of using the present system of separate trains. At the 'stations' of the new system the passengers would step on to a type of escalator which gradually accelerates from walking pace to the speed of the transporter.

Such are some of the more advanced types of transport that have been proposed for cities before the end of this century. Equally startling suggestions have been made for the roads of the future. Here the main changes may be expected in the vehicles rather than in the road itself. It seems that the motor-car in some form or another is here to stay; the advantages of this individualised transport mode, able to provide a door-to-door service precisely as required, are too great to be surrendered. The rise in the car-owning population must be expected to continue, therefore; by the year 2000, in the United States, there will be more cars than people. This prospect will force a number of changes in the design of cars that will make them virtually unrecognisable. The electrically powered car will become virtually universal, and the tendency to smaller and smaller town cars will continue until they are little more than silent cubes (*see* Plate 29). These may be designed to carry only one person, though probably by the end of the century they will have multi-purpose bodies to carry a larger number of passengers for country use. Wheels will become progressively smaller; by the year 2000 most vehicles will be using the hovercraft principle or some form of magnetic suspension. In this, the car will be kept hovering above the road surface by the mutual repulsion between a continuous magnet in the road and an opposed one in the car. To keep the two magnets poised one above the other, the car will probably be held to the centre of the road by some kind of guide rail. Apart from this, friction will have been entirely eliminated and the emergency braking system will be virtually foolproof, a simple matter of turning off the electric current in the solenoid providing the magnetic field in the car.

To the possibility that the road itself may provide part of the suspension of the car must be added the likelihood that it will also provide the motive power of the vehicle. Developments in the field of linear motors make it probable that in the not-too-distant future the principle may be applied to road transport, particularly in the larger towns.

Let us now turn to the certainties of future plans for traffic control. As the density of traffic on roads of all types increases, systems of automatic computerised remote control will undoubtedly be applied to the field of private vehicular transport as one already is, in a limited sense, to the trains of London's Underground. The driver of the future will probably still have to get his car from his own front door to the nearest main road, but there he will join a convoy of vehicles and gear his drive mechanism into the central automatic system. This will supervise the traffic and literally drive it; the standard motorway of the future will have from four to six lanes in both directions, as many in America already have. These lanes will be restricted to various types of traffic and each lane will have its own specific speed limit. The vehicles will travel in batches of from fifteen to twenty, spaced at ten-feet intervals, and with twenty-yard gaps between each batch to allow for breakdowns and for vehicles wishing to change lane or leave the motorway. In this production-line progress through the countryside, the 'driver' will be free to relax in any way he chooses, reading a book, catching up on office work, playing chess with his passenger or making a telephone call. His only concern will be to notify the central system of future turn-offs that he needs to make. Presumably in a still more advanced future, when the whole network of major and secondary roads have been rebuilt for such computerised control, the driver will simply need to feed a programme for his whole journey on the major network into a computer when he first joins the motorway, and then settle back until an alarm call notifies him that he has reached the required exit point. In ancient India a driver was absolved of responsibility for an accident if he had shouted a warning to the other fool to get out of the way. In the futuristic world of the planners there will be no accidents and, one assumes, no shouting—unless it transpires that even computers lose patience sorting out endless traffic jams.

It is assumed that even by the end of the century in the more advanced industrial countries about one-third of the vehicles will still be powered by internal combustion engines, but their users will be ever more heavily penalised both by higher and higher fuel taxes and limitations on their freedom of movement. If mankind lives long enough to see the brave new world here being described, he will find himself battling against steep odds to salvage from his polluted habitat some environment in which continued life will be, if not enjoyable, at least possible.

There are some indications that the menace is already beginning to be appreciated and the warnings acted upon. In the future, laws to control atmospheric pollution will become even more stringent, as will laws to prevent degradation of the environment by noise and other nuisance. For town driving it is probable that the rechargeable battery motor will be the only form of prime mover permitted until the road itself provides the motive power. In the country, while the messy and expensive internal combustion engine car may remain a status symbol, most drivers will prefer to use an engine powered by the fuel cells at present being developed, while for the sports car enthusiast there will be various types of gas turbine cars. In all parts of the traffic system speed limits will be carefully regulated and automatically enforced, but they will represent actual speeds, and the real speed of all traffic will be increased by as much as a factor of four.

Nothing that has been described in this chapter is in any sense impossible technically; indeed, given the necessary capital investment, much could be implemented now. However, for our purposes, it is perhaps more interesting to notice how, even in the most remote and exciting speculations on the pattern of road travel in the future, basic principles that we have seen operating throughout the history of road-building, continue to influence design and to lie at the root of thinking on the subject. No matter how advanced technology may become, both the function of the road and the nature of the traffic it is designed to bear will continue to be determining factors. The classic conflict of the eighteenth century between adapting the vehicle to suit the road or adapting the road to suit the traffic will be neatly resolved in the future, when these two elements will achieve an almost symbiotic relationship.

Book List

ASHWORTH, ROBERT. *Highway Engineering* (Heinemann Educational Books), 1966

BATSON, R. G. (2nd edition, J. A. PROUDLOVE). *Roads* (Longmans), 1968

BIRD, ANTHONY. *Roads and Vehicles* (Longmans), 1969

BUCHANAN, PROFESSOR COLIN. *Traffic in Towns* (H.M.S.O.; Penguin), 1963

CROWE, SYLVIA. *The Landscape of Roads* (Architectural Press), 1960

DE CAMP, L. SPRAGUE. *Ancient Engineers* (Souvenir Press), 1963

FORBES, R. J. *Notes on the History of Ancient Roads and their Construction* (Adolf M. Hakkert), 1964

HALPRIN, LAWRENCE. *Freeways* (Reinhold), 1966

MARGARY, IVAN. *Roman Roads in Britain* (Baker), revised edition, 1967

MERRICK, HUGH. *The Great Motor Highways of the Alps* (Hale), 1961

MOONEY, W. W. *Travel Among the Ancient Romans*, 1920

MUMBY, DENYS (Ed.). *Transport Selected Readings* (Penguin), 1968

OGLESBY, C. H. and HEWES, L. I. *Highway Engineering* (Wiley), 2nd edition, 1964

OVERMAN, MICHAEL. *Roads, Bridges and Tunnels* (Aldus), 1968

ROBERTSON, ALAN W. *Great Britain's Post Roads, Post Towns and Postal Rates 1635–1839* (Robertson), 1961

ROLT, L. T. C. *Thomas Telford* (Longmans), 1958

SCHREIBER, HERMANN (translated by Stewart Thompson). *The History of Roads* (Barrie & Rockliff), 1961

THOMPSON, J. MICHAEL. *Motorways in London*, Report of a Working Party of the London Amenity and Transport Association (Duckworth), 1969

Urban Motorways, A Report of the London Conference organised by the British Road Federation (British Road Federation), 1956

VON HAGEN, VICTOR W. *Roman Roads* (Weidenfeld and Nicolson), 1967

Index